Praise for The No-Nonsense Guide to
Green Parenting:

"This is an inspiring and practical book which will be of great interest to every parent who wants their children to have the kind of childhood they deserve."

Sir Christopher Woodhead, *Sunday Times* **columnist and former chief inspector of schools**

"For most of us parenting is a joy but also a pretty significant challenge! So helping to create the next generation of wildlife lovers in today's world, in an eco-friendly way, can seem all but impossible. Not now. This book is packed full of green ideas and great ways to inspire your kids about nature, how to drag them away from the screens and feel great as you watch their eyes light up with the joy of the natural world."

Stephanie Hilborne OBE, chief executive of The Wildlife Trusts

"This book contains a wealth of ideas and inspiration for green parenting. Alongside advice on why to choose a more natural approach there are practical ways for you to get started right away at home. What I love is how many projects there are for the whole family. Make your own bath bombs or create a mini meadow in a window box, for example. I love the section on foraging stuffed with seasonal recipes. Kate has created challenges, which appear throughout the book and encourage every member of the family to choose a greener, more meaningful existence. Dive in to this rich resource and have fun going green!"

Melissa Corkhill, editor of The Green Parent magazine, www.thegreenparent.co.uk

"Kate has a great way of understanding and interpreting nature and the natural world coupled with a true sense of sustainability and a real understanding of parenthood. This is a book packed full of ideas and helpful suggestions – a must for parents and children alike. I love the way it is written and its so inspiring to think of both forgotten and new ways of engaging with daily tasks. This is a true guide to making a difference and adding value to our children and the planet."

Richard Powell OBE, lifelong environmental and heritage conservationist including 24 years with the RSPB

"It's not just a big, bright, colourful manual on how to have fun with all the family, this book carries a vitally important message that connecting kids to nature is critical for the future of our planet. The No-Nonsense Guide to Green Parenting is as necessary as it is timely."

Mark Cocker, naturalist, environmental activist and author of Birds Britannica

"At last – a good parenting guide which doesn't make you feel inadequate! Kate Blincoe shows how green parenting is not about hairshirts or home-made muesli but blends convenient modern technology with healthier, greener alternatives. This book is full of realistic tips for being greener around the home and brilliant ideas for wild play, from teddy dens to lawn letters. You'll see how greener parenting is more fun for your children – and more fun for you. I'm a nature-loving parent still struggling with screens, plastic toys and supermarket food, and Kate's simple, inspiring ideas and good sense is just what I need."

Patrick Barkham, author of *Coastlines* and *The Butterfly Isles*

"So much in this book that I wish I knew when my children were small. A fabulous resource for new -– and not so new – parents!"

Sara Parkin, founder director, Forum for the Future

"Imaginative and practical, inspiring yet down-to-earth, Kate Blincoe's lively, easy-to-read book offers busy parents a wealth of simple and insightful ideas to help them provide their children with a nurturing and balanced childhood. Following her guidance will help parents to bring up their children to be enthusiastically in tune with the natural world and to handle some of the challenges of contemporary technology."

Dr. Teresa Belton, founder member of Play for Life and author of *Happier People Healthier Planet*

"I wish I had written this book! It echoes so many of my feelings about modern-day parenting. Full of inspired ideas and practical methods to get 'back to nature' in the modern world. Anyone wanting to find alternatives to screens and electronics should read this book."

Miranda Krestovnikoff, television and radio broadcaster, BBC's Coast and The One Show

"This is the ultimate handbook for a fun, green and healthy family. I love this book. It is inspirational and uplifting and will help any family reconnect with nature. A balanced and healthy lifestyle, with free-range, active kids is the secret wonder-product the ad men don't want you to know about. It leaves the TV and plastic toys standing. So get out there and try these great ideas."

David Bond, director of Project Wild Thing and The Wild Network

The **No-Nonsense Guide** to
Green Parenting

How to raise your child, help save the planet and not go mad

Kate Blincoe

Published by
Green Books
An imprint of UIT Cambridge Ltd
www.greenbooks.co.uk

PO Box 145, Cambridge CB4 1GQ, England
+44 (0) 1223 302 041

First published in England in 2016

Kate Blincoe has asserted her moral rights under the
Copyright, Designs and Patents Act 1988.

Photographs by Phil Barnes, www.philbarnes-commercialphotography.co.uk, unless listed below.
Photographs by James Williamson, www.norfolknaturesafari.co.uk, on pages 27, 44, 91, 92, 121,
122 (teasels), 125, 130 (ragged robin), 133, 137, 144 (sparrow), 146 (fox), 148, 149, 151, 152, 156,
168, 170, 173, 174, 176 and 177.
Photographs pages 9 © Ant Jones (cliqq.co.uk), 88 by the author, 119 © Vvoennyy via 123rf.com
and 129 © Michael Lane via 123rf.com.

All illustrations, garden designs and the paintings in Chapter 2 by Stephanie Laurence.

Design by Mad-i-Creative
www.mad-i-creative.co.uk

ISBN: 978 0 85784 254 1 (paperback)
ISBN: 978 0 85784 255 8 (ePub)
ISBN: 978 0 85784 256 5 (PDF)
Also available for Kindle.

With all outdoor activities, or indeed most scenarios involving little people, there can be a small
degree of risk. Please use your common sense and judgement to ensure the safety of your children. Make
sure you go on a first-aid course and take your charged mobile phone with you on all your adventures.

Disclaimer: the advice herein is believed to be correct at
the time of printing, but the author and publisher accept
no liability for actions inspired by this book.

10 9 8 7 6 5 4 3 2 1

For Sam and Annie

Contents

Foreword by
Nikki Duffy

It is so often the case that the modern quest for 'green-ness' is characterized by negativity. It's set up as a high and holy goal, a hopeless ideal that we are all doomed to fall far short of. The narrow way to eco-friendliness is paved with admonition and, for a project rooted in the best possible intentions, it's frightening how easily trying to be green becomes all about guilt and a sense of failure.

When you think about it, you could say exactly the same thing about modern parenting – in our culture at least. How often are we made to feel ashamed, whether by ourselves or others, for our shortcomings as parents? How rarely do we allow ourselves to celebrate what we do, what we get right, what we achieve, and to grasp the challenges of raising children as the messy, mixed-up but ultimately hope-filled riot that they are? I speak as someone with a post-grad degree in Parental Anxiety and Guilt (that's made-up, by the way, but only just) but one thing I have clung to since the day my first daughter was born is that, with children, you can always start afresh. Each day is a new day. They will forgive you. You can forgive yourself. And then you can move on. You will almost certainly make some interesting new cock-ups today – but you will also, simultaneously, do some really cool, grade-A parenting.

That is the spirit of hope, generosity, pragmatism and optimism in which Kate Blincoe has written this book, and that's why it is so lovely to read.

Kate communicates as someone who is striving, not preaching, who's standing side by side with her reader, not delivering advice from on-high – but who also, handily, has some extremely good ideas that you probably hadn't thought of and that will make your journey towards sustainable living a lot easier and more fun.

I love the abundance of sane, practical suggestions throughout the book – particularly Kate's advice on shopping, cooking and avoiding food waste, subjects close to my own heart. I've taken a real shine to Grumpy Granny and her not-always-comfortable but nevertheless thought-provoking points. And, alongside the many brilliant new ideas, I'm smugly pleased to find there are things in these pages that I can say I am already doing. I'm certain most readers will find the same. This book isn't about something that's very hard to achieve, it's about organizing, motivating and being creative: channeling the good will towards the world that we surely all possess into real, concrete, planet-friendly living. What a breath of fresh air.

Nikki Duffy is a freelance food writer and author of *The River Cottage Baby and Toddler Cookbook.* She was formerly deputy editor of the award-winning magazine *Waitrose Food Illustrated* and wrote a weekly food column in the *Guardian.* Nikki is a keen advocate of breastfeeding, baby-led weaning and a seasonal, wholefood diet for children, alongside a healthy, outdoorsy lifestyle – but also believes strongly that trying to be perfect will probably send you mad and that parents should relax, trust their instincts and just do the best they can. Nikki lives in Essex with her two beautiful daughters, who wish they were allowed tomato ketchup a bit more often.

About the author

Kate's passion for the environment began at a young age. Growing up on a farm, she was often to be found eating soil and worms or playing in a stream. As a fifteen year old, Kate began a monthly opinion column for the local paper focusing on countryside and farming topics, such as the hunting debate and GM foods.

Kate is a combination of a writer who likes science or a scientist who likes writing. As a result she studied English Literature at the University of East Anglia and then went on to do a Graduate Diploma in Environmental Science. Still attached to university life she accepted a job in academia, carrying out studies in environmental epidemiology and environmental economics and writing papers for scientific journals.

Kate learnt the hard graft of paying attention to a high level of detail and was successful in this role but the creative, outdoors side of her personality was unfulfilled. Nature called to her and she left to work in environmental education for the RSPB, coordinating environmental education and family events across the Eastern region of England.

Kate soon noticed that the children on field trips to RSPB nature reserves often had little experience of nature and the countryside. They were sometimes scared of going in the woods. It was only when they got stuck in that they relaxed and started to have fun, learning about the world around them. Kids seen as the rowdy or difficult ones in the classroom often became entranced and absorbed – their teachers would be stunned! It became clear to Kate that nature and children needed each other.

Next, Kate became the RSPB's regional communication manager, committed to sharing her passion for nature and the environment with everyone. She quickly learnt that a personal angle and humour could help people engage with complex topics such as biodiversity loss or climate change, when before they may have said 'that's not for me'.

Kate became increasingly green in her lifestyle, with lots of cycling to work, organic vegetables and carbon counting. Then … she had two children. Life became about survival and staying awake while driving her screaming baby around the block to soothe him to sleep. Meals became about what a teething infant would eat rather than what heritage vegetable was available. Being green wasn't so easy anymore.

Her post-child sanity was achieved through walks in the countryside and visits to her father's farm. A spin off from this was that her growing kids became gradually more connected and engaged with the wild world around them. Kate realised that as a parent, she needed to redefine her concept of 'green' to include a hands-on love and understanding of nature.

Now, Kate is a freelance writer, specialising in sustainability and the environment, but always with a passion for encouraging children to get outdoors and use all five senses to explore their world.

The grass is greener outside

Introduction

If you were hoping for a guide on how to grow a hair shirt before the whole family (baby included) cycle 20 miles to the allotment, then this probably isn't the book for you. This is a book for the rest of us. We are the 'a bit knackered but still care about the world' brigade, and the 'I used to bike everywhere, but since having the kids I bought a people carrier' club.

We all know a fair bit about how to be green, but goodness me doesn't it seem hard to apply to your life once you're a parent? The volume of washing massively increases and you need to transport your children to various clubs and play dates. You may also want the house a little warmer in winter and your priority is them eating some vegetables, not necessarily whether their food is in season. Not only that, but when you are feeling tired it is easy to opt for the electronic babysitter.

Underneath the fatigue and busyness, we believe in free-range eggs and free-range children. We want our little ones to spend time outside getting muddy and to spot that tiny wren before it pops back into the undergrowth. We want to know that, despite it all, we have done our best to make sure our teenage children don't turn round and say 'thanks for trashing the planet as well as giving me your nose / frizzy hair / fear of spiders'.

Doing the right thing for the environment is invariably the right thing for your child. From the air they breathe and the food they eat to the nature that inspires them, our children are far more connected to the world around them than we realize. Low carbon is important, but it is only one part of bringing up green children. Nature and the outdoors should be at the heart of it because they are vital for everyone's mental well-being as well as our physical health and fitness.

Unless the next generation can understand and feel part of the natural world, they will not know how to truly care for it or be equipped to make sound environmental choices. We must prepare them for the challenges ahead.

This book is about having some fun, being realistic and making the values you have a bit easier to fit into the busy world of family life. There is no one-size-fits-all way of being green, so dip in, see what takes your fancy, laugh at your failings and try again.

Learn and play naturally

Time and space to explore

1

My small hands reach around rough bark, grasping for a hold. My foot flexes as it adjusts position to feel more secure in its nook. I focus my eyes upwards on the branch just out of reach. Can I manage it? Will I slip...? A quick stretch and I've got it! Now I can pull myself up higher than Daddy's head, and I feel safe and proud here in my tree.

What has this child just learnt? So much, including concentration, determination, bravery, risk assessment, how to develop gross and fine motor skills and understanding the power of their own body. This was all from the simple act of climbing a tree, a free activity that is available near you, right now.

Children have a lot to learn to equip them for school. I'm not talking about the alphabet or how to scrawl their name, but rather how to manage their own bodies and emotions, as well as how to engage with others and be able to assess dangers for themselves.

There are magical activities that teach all this through play. They include cooking, gardening, reading together and being outdoors. These are simple old-fashioned pleasures that can get forgotten in our technology-filled world. Not only that, but play has been proven to develop clever children[1] and help them do well at school.

Play can be seen as something trivial that lacks purpose, something to merely pass the time until a child becomes a productive citizen. In fact, a child cannot learn how to become a fully rounded adult without play.

Technology has changed play and leisure dramatically in the last 30 years. With on-demand TV and tailored programming, gone is the concept of waiting for your favourite weekly show. Add our ever-present phones, tablets and online gaming and it is clear that we have become accustomed to instant gratification. Alongside this, our children are exposed to constant advertising selling increasingly gender-based toys and lifestyles.

This chapter is about stepping back from our technology and away from the consumerist urges that increase our impact on the environment. It is about simple yet creative play that allows children to learn in the very best way … naturally and often accidentally.

Seek out toys made from wood

The toy mountain

Chances are you have a toy mountain in your home. It may be Everest-sized or a more modest Kilimanjaro. It may be confined to one room (I wish) or spread willy-nilly around your home. Either way, it matters to the environment exactly how your toy mountain is created and managed.

What's it made from?

For eco-toys, we all know that wood is the way forward. It is the best choice for the environment because plastic contains oil-based petrochemicals and won't biodegrade in landfill. There is often a wooden alternative to plastic dominoes, building blocks, digger tractors, tools. Tactile, more durable and undeniably more attractive, wood will pass the 'hand me on' test long after plastic toys have broken. Wooden toys can be more expensive, but because they last so well can often be found secondhand.

Also look out for toys made from other renewable substances, such as natural rubber, organic cotton, wool or plant-based bioplastics. Avoiding plastic altogether is nearly impossible, so choose durable, quality plastic that will last for years – for example, Lego is practically indestructible. Make sure you opt for one of the safer kinds of plastic, with fewer harmful chemicals. These will be labelled with a 2, 4 or 5 in the pet symbol. For the best safety standards, check it is British-made and free from Bisphenol A (BPA) – an industrial chemical. Some toys are made from recycled plastic, such as old milk cartons.

Where is it made?

All toys sold across Europe must conform to strict safety regulations, but there have been instances of imported toys being recalled. Look for manufacturers based in the UK to reduce the air miles on your products and ensure high ethical standards. If buying from abroad, check that it is a Fairtrade item.

Be aware that imported toys may contain lead. It is used in paint and plastic to enhance flexibility. Even low levels of lead in children's blood have been shown to affect IQ, the ability to pay attention and academic achievement.[2]

Can I buy it secondhand?

The beauty of used items is that they have a much lower impact on the planet. Try eBay, Gumtree, Preloved or Freecycle and don't forget the charity shops in your high street, or National Childbirth Trust sales (anyone can go – you don't have to be a member).

Buying secondhand can save you time too. Take a wooden playhouse or cabin bed, for example. Instead of having to construct one from zillions of panels of flat-pack, you may only need to break it down a little to transport it.

Is it Green or Gross...

to forget to clean your toys after friends come round? (Or, like, ever?)

Even a smelly old sock can become a little friend with some basic sewing and imagination!

Can I make it?

Homemade toys may sound a bit 1950s, but it is the creations that children have had a hand in that really capture their imagination. Most household rubbish can be reused to make exciting toys to occupy an afternoon – bean-filled shakers, water-bottle rockets, cereal-box masks, cardboard-box cars and trains. And that odd sock is just crying out to be a puppet. When they've had enough, just recycle it.

Sensory bottles for baby (six months onwards)

Clear-plastic water bottles filled with different household objects will intrigue and delight your little one. Aim for a mix of sounds and colours for maximum impact.

You will need:

4 or so clear-plastic bottles – the small 250ml or 330ml ones are ideal for little hands

a few of these items: buttons, pebbles, dried beans, dry rice, beads, tin foil, water, food colouring, washing-up liquid, baby oil, golden syrup, pipe cleaners, cut-up drinking straws, sand

gaffer tape

Simply fill each bottle with a variety of objects, such as tin-foil balls, water and blue food colouring; or pipe cleaners and dried beans; or golden syrup, baby oil, water and red food colouring. For best results, leave at least a third of the bottle empty so it can all swish around. Seal the bottle carefully, using gaffer tape over the lid.

Gooey silly putty for pre-schoolers

This stuff is like Play-Doh but more mouldable. You can alter the consistency by changing the amount of Epsom salts you add – less for a gunkier, stickier feel and more for a firmer pliable texture which will bounce if made into a ball, or copy newsprint off a newspaper.

(Older children may be interested to learn that this is a process called polymerisation, whereby small molecules join together to make long ones. Handy knowledge for GCSE science.)

You will need:

- ½ tsp Epsom salts
- ½ tsp water
- 2 small cups or bowls
- food colouring
- 1 tbsp white glue
- a craft stick for stirring

This makes an egg-sized portion of putty ideal for one child to play with. Simply multiply the recipe for more. Stir the salts into the water in a small cup or bowl until it has mostly dissolved (it may not do so completely). Add in a few drops of food colouring. Now add this mixture to your glue in another bowl and stir with the craft stick until it becomes mouldable.

Store in a sealed pot in the fridge – it should last for a few months. For easy tidying up, play with it on greaseproof paper.

Eco skipping rope for older children

However hard you try, plastic bags have a habit of accumulating. This is a fun way of using them up, but you could also use old T-shirts or jeans. If your child hasn't mastered skipping yet, then this is perfect for a tug of war.

You will need:

- 12 plastic carrier bags
- scissors
- gaffer tape

Cut open the plastic bags open so they are flat, then cut off the handles so that you are left with a rectangle of plastic. Now cut this rectangle into long, roughly even strips, about 5-10cm wide.

Tie the strips together to make a length that is about 20cm longer than your required skipping rope and trim off any excess plastic sticking out from the knots. When you have 12 lengths ready, tie half of them to a chair (or get someone to hold them firmly). Plait these six lengths together.

Repeat for the other six. Now firmly twist the two plaits together and tape each end to form the handles.

Battery power

So many modern toys require batteries, so invest in a charger for reusable batteries, or look out for toys that don't use batteries, such as friction toys.

Choose a few items to swap with a friend

Toy swap

Kids seem bored of their toys? That's not a reason to buy more. Arranging to swap a few items with a friend for a week or so can work really well. The key is to prepare your child for this – there is nothing like enforced swapping to make a child feel possessive.

Many libraries have toy sections where, for a small fee, you can borrow toys to take home. Look out too for toy libraries organized by local councils offering anything from baby walkers to digger trucks.

When you're done

Pass unwanted toys on or sell them online or at a car-boot sale. Your local playgroup may be interested in toys and books if they are in good condition.

Quiet the consumer monster

Following Christmas and birthdays, the mood in our children tends to shift. There are too many toys and an undeniable sense of entitlement: a growing belief that the constant acquisition of presents should be a normal state of affairs, not a twice-yearly luxury.

We can't escape our material world; indeed it brings us many pleasures. But with a little thought our children can grow up mindful of their privileges. If you're interested in learning more about how consumption impacts both on the environment and our well-being, *Happier People Healthier Planet* by Teresa Belton is a thought-provoking read.

Brilliant
books

Let's be honest, books are amazing (even when you've read them 10,000 times, damn you *The Very Hungry Caterpillar*). If there is one thing I would recommend you spoil your children with (apart from time outdoors and your attention) it would be books.

Reading, wherever you are, will take you to a new place ...without the carbon footprint

Here is my pick of the loveliest reads that will help inspire a love of nature, wildlife and care of the planet in your kids. They are perfect for whiling away some time under the shade of a beautiful willow tree by a river somewhere (or while perching together in a grim airport waiting for your delayed flight, hoping to make yourself feel better about the air miles).

Books for younger children

- A mini-beast identification book, with colourful drawings, photographs and a spotter's tick list – such as the *RSPB First Book of Mini-beasts* by Anita Ganeri and David Chandler.
- *The Lorax* by Dr Seuss – a tale of the wonder of nature and the way humanity can threaten it.
- All Eric Carle books but particularly *The Tiny Seed*. It shows the massive challenges faced by nature to simply survive. Why not plant your own seed after reading it?
- *Are You a Ladybird?* by Judy Allen and Tudor Humphries – this beautifully illustrated book has an amusing way of telling the story of the ladybird's life cycle. It is also a good springboard for thinking about why creatures are different from one another and what role they all play in the environment.
- *Follow the Swallow* by Julia Donaldson and Pam Smy tells the amazing tale of migration in an entertaining, readable style.
- *The Utterly Otterleys* by Mairi Hedderwick – the Utterly Otterley family live in a cosy burrow near the river, where everything is just about perfect. Then Pa Utterly Otterley wakes up one morning and decides it's time to find a new home. Enchanting illustrations take you to wildest Scotland and the story can lead to good chats about what different animals need for their homes.
- *A First Book of Nature* by Nicola Davies – part poetry, part scrapbook of recipes, facts and fragments. The stunning artwork by Mark Hearld brings magic and excitement to the natural world. This book is great for pre-schoolers as well as early primary.

Books for older children

- Children's bird-watching guide – look for one with some easy-to-recognize species, and buy some good children's binoculars.
- *Nick Baker's Bug Book* – did you know that some species of snail are hairy? This book is full of quirky facts and will encourage an understanding of all types of insects found in our back gardens and beyond.
- *The RSPB Children's Guide to Nature Watching* by Mark Boyd – from dolphins to deer, there is a world of nature waiting to be discovered. This book will be your companion as well as providing an identification guide to common species.
- *How the Whale Became and Other Stories* by Ted Hughes – accessible and funny stories for children of five-plus which will encourage them to think about how creatures such as bees, hares and polar bears have evolved.
- *The Nature Explorer's Handbook: How to make friends with snails and other creatures* by Moira Butterfield – this fun and action-packed book will inspire children to get outside. Kids will enjoy the record-breakers and a spotter's guide to the creatures they can find locally.
- *Will Jellyfish Rule the World?* by Leo Hickman – this book breaks down the causes and effects of climate change into fresh, fun and easy-to-follow questions and answers, with lots of ideas for taking action.
- *Magical Animals at Bedtime* by Lou Kuenzler and Sandra Rigby – like modern Aesop's Fables, these beautiful tales will help your child navigate life with morals inspired by the natural world.

Top 10 ways to ... prevent spoiled brats

1. After an influx of gifts, ask your child to find three old toys to give away to charity shops.

2. Ask grandparents and close relatives to save the treats for special occasions or to encourage children to earn them – for example by washing the car or watering the plants.

3. Record favourite programmes and fast-forward the ads.

4. Handwritten thank-you letters are a must (or picture thank-you cards for younger children).

5. Occasionally (and for no reason at all) give them random cost-free gifts: perhaps a shoebox filled with old spare photos or a beautiful stone you found on the beach. This mirrors the behaviour of many pre-schoolers who might present you with a daisy or a half-chewed biscuit as if they were bestowing great riches. Tell them where you found it or how you made it, and why you think it is special. Don't feel the need to give identical gifts if you have more than one child – find something that you think each individual will appreciate.

6. Help them wrap up their toys in old scraps of wrapping paper, magazine pages, or brown paper which is hardy and recyclable, then have imaginary parties where they pretend to give toys to friends, siblings or even to their teddies. The emphasis is on pretend gifting and role-play – make it clear they are not really giving away their treasured items but taking turns to share them. Alternatively, they could package up their favourite toys for themselves, which encourages them to see their current possessions as gifts.

7. Teach the value of money. All children should contribute to household jobs, but there are tasks over and above making their bed and laying the table that can be rewarded with a pound or two. This could be sorting the laundry or weeding the flower bed – whatever would help you and they are capable of. Understanding that we work for money will help them to appreciate its worth. Then let them buy whatever they want with their hard-earned cash, but highlight the importance of saving up for something they really want.

8. Stand firm in the supermarket or sweeties and magazines will feel like their entitlement. Say no twice and you will break the cycle. Instead, let them choose interesting fruit or vegetables you don't usually buy as their reward for coming shopping with you, and find a suitable recipe together.

9. Try not to be too impulsive, or generous, when shopping for yourself with the children.

10. Teach them a make-do-and-mend attitude by repairing toys and clothes rather than just chucking broken things straight in the bin.

Green art and craft

The most eco-friendly craft projects are those which use household recycling items, food and objects gathered from nature. These can include pasta art, milk-bottle lids with a pine cone affixed and decorated, leaf prints, bark rubbing, collages out of birthday cards and sewing projects using outgrown clothes.

Of course, you will also need to buy certain items to help create and decorate the many works of art. Source beeswax plasticine, air-drying modelling clay, paints made from natural earth pigments or foodstuffs, wooden beads, plant-dyed felt, recycled tissue paper and crayons containing beeswax (usually combined with paraffin). You can also find eco-glues that are safe for children: look for those containing natural ingredients such as citric acid and rice flour.

Consumerism you can do without

Shop-bought smoothies

They are packed full of sugar and often overpriced. Make your own healthier version with hidden vegetables, or stick to water.

See in the dark smoothies

Serves 3-4

This bright-orange smoothie is packed full of beta-carotene for healthy eyes.

You will need:

350ml almond milk (or cow's milk)

2 carrots, peeled and chopped

180g fresh mango chunks

1 frozen banana

Simply blend the ingredients together until smooth. Add a little more milk for a thinner consistency. If you don't have time to freeze a banana, you could add a couple of ice cubes.

Buggy boards

These make for lazy kids. Just allow more time to get to where you need to go. Children should be able to walk or scoot half a mile and back from the age of three.

Colour-coded toys

Manufacturers frequently produce feminized versions of their best sellers. We all know that boys like playing kitchens and girls like playing with building blocks, so buy rainbow colours if possible to save money and keep everyone happy.

Flavoured water in a bottle

Use reusable bottles to fill at home from the tap. The mineral levels of some bottled waters make them unsuitable for young children anyway.

Put away your cotton wool

Helicopter parents tend to hover over their children, intervening in their every move and twitching to catch them at the tiniest stumble. They always decide for the child whether an activity is safe or not.

The opposite of helicopter parenting is sometimes called under-parenting and it could help you avoid producing a cosseted 'cotton-wool kid'. It is about giving children some age-appropriate space (both emotional and physical) to explore their world and learn about risk for themselves. A safe outdoors space in which to have adventures is essential, but whether that is your garden or the park, it's a chance for you to let them make decisions and sort out the squabbles themselves, while remaining watchful.

This laid-back style of parenting is surprisingly hard to do, because it is challenging not to intervene when there is a risk of minor bumps or during disagreements between friends or siblings. Children who are used to

Give your children a little physical and emotional space whenever you can parents watching over them can feel a bit clingy at first as they adapt to making their own choices and mistakes. All this time though they are learning about risk, independence, their environment and how to negotiate with others.

Special
educational needs

Natural settings have so much to offer for children with autistic spectrum disorders, or behavioural or physical difficulties. As with all kids, the space and fresh air can improve their sense of well-being and lead to more exercise and a release of tension. It has been found that children with ADHD who play in green spaces exhibit less severe symptoms than those who only play in 'hard' landscapes or indoors.[3]

Outdoor activities can show a whole new side to their personality, as well as help with making friends and improving social skills.[4] Not only that, but children with special needs often learn best through doing, so being outside can give them the opportunity to get involved with more practical activities.[5] During outdoor education sessions that I have run over the years, I would often notice how intently engaged a child was in pond dipping or working out which mini-beast they had found. Frequently the child's teacher or parent would reveal that the child could barely concentrate for a moment in the classroom.

You don't need an organized excursion to a nature reserve to gain these benefits; simple gardening activities have been shown to be highly valuable (see Chapter 6).

Top 5 tips for ... under-parenting

1. Set them a task with a reward attached, such as building the world's tallest Lego tower to gain 20 minutes of telly time, or finding a living creature for 10 minutes more story time before bed. Older children could climb a tree to earn a chocolate biscuit. Then withdraw and leave them to get on with it. This will focus their minds and encourage independent thought and teamwork.

2. Be invisible but present. Can you spy from the kitchen window or listen from the next room to check all is well, but give them the impression they are all by themselves?

3. Ignore dirt and snot slugs. Don't fuss over them with tissues and wipes while they are still happily playing.

4. Give them a chance to work things out for themselves before you holler 'Try the steps' or 'That's too high'.

5. If they get hurt, don't criticize their actions. They will have learnt something new and probably just need a cuddle instead. Try not to feel guilty either.

The role
of schools

In an ideal world, schools would take the lead on outdoor education, but in practice this varies massively and can be limited by factors such as staff confidence or the availability of green space. Ultimately most schools' priority is helping children to pass exams and maintain their Ofsted rating. As a result, schools vary greatly in the level of outdoors education they can offer.

This can present challenges for the green parent. Do you choose the good local school that you can walk to (pluses: within your community, offering the chance to nature-spot with your child, low-carbon footprint) or do you drive to the school with the nature garden and lots of outside space? Whatever your school's level of eco-awareness, you can support their nature work.

You could…

- fundraise for and coordinate the creation (and crucially the maintenance) of a nature garden at school;
- become a parent governor and highlight the importance of outdoors time built into lesson plans;
- discuss forest schools with your child's head teacher;
- lobby your MP to keep topics such as climate change on the curriculum;
- keep a watchful eye on your school's playing field and fight tooth and nail if it is under threat (in an alarming trend in recent years, one school playing field is sold off every three weeks!)[6];
- suggest days out to local nature reserves. Many will have tailored outdoor education programmes that will help schools meet learning targets as well as provide an inspirational day out. The RSPB and Wildlife Trusts are worth a look.

Walk to school

According to official figures, during rush hour one in five cars is on the school run – removing just half of them would make a massive difference to slashing carbon emissions and air pollution. You'll save money too – did you know that the average school run costs over £400 a year?[7]

Not only that, the walk is a lovely chance to chat and experience the changing seasons and spot wildlife (however urban your route). Walking to school can also help your child build independence, road-safety awareness and social skills.

Why not ask your school how it encourages walking to school, and lobby your local council to introduce 20mph zones and traffic-calming measures in your area?

If you live too far to walk, then park safely a distance away from that school gate chaos and enjoy a stroll.

Learning on the go

Wherever you are – on the train, driving through countryside or wandering around the shops – there is a chance for your child to observe and learn about the world around them.

Green [CHALLENGE] #1

Litter picking is a brilliant activity for learning about our impact on the planet. It also prompts discussion about packaging, how we can avoid it and what we should do with it. Safety and supervision are requirements here along with gloves and warnings about sharp items. You can buy kid-size litter pickers or join an organized litter pick in your community or at beach-tidy events.

Try this spotter's game

One point per spot, first to get five wins!

Can you spot...

- a gull (there is no such thing as a seagull but many different types of gull, such as the herring gull, black-headed gull, and so on)
- a pigeon (you can talk about how well pigeons have adapted to city life and why they have managed it when some other creatures haven't)
- a wind turbine (and does your child understand how it works?)
- an electrically powered vehicle (for example, an electric bus or a Toyota Prius)
- a shop with its front door open in cold weather (wasting precious energy – go and tell them off)
- a traffic jam (discuss what causes congestion on the road)
- a tractor (ask your child why a tractor goes slower than a car)
- a mammal (how will your child know that they are a mammal?)
- some litter (which could lead into a conversation about the importance of recycling)
- an oak tree (you could talk about what makes an oak tree so special that it is many countries' national tree).

Photo safari

Letting your child use a camera can transform a simple walk. Ask them to take photos of the things they are interested in and then help them make an album or diary of their adventure. The child's-eye view of the world is enchantingly different to the adult's. Recording their experience encourages a child to really look at their surroundings.

Make up outdoorsy stories

Many of us already tell our children made-up stories and it can be lovely to introduce an outdoors or nature-based theme. Children's lives are fairly restricted by traffic and safety, but in an imaginary world you can place them in all sorts of crazy situations. Lost pets and animals in peril make a good starting point. You are likely to end up with talking creatures, so perfect your rabbit voice!

My children love stories about a baby squirrel named Squinky who gets in all sorts of scrapes, loves bubble baths and riding in their rucksacks, and frequently needs rescuing.

Green [CHALLENGE] #2

Under many roads are secret tunnels for streams to pass underneath. These can be fantastic fun for climbing in and actually going under the road. You will feel like you have discovered subterranean caves.

Just keep your eyes open when driving along country lanes, as there are hundreds of these tunnels to be found. If you haven't spotted any while going about your daily business, have a look on an OS map. Look for a stream that vanishes as it bisects a road and appears on the other side. Avoid raging rivers; this is all about little streams.

Do wear wellies and waterproofs and don't go in after heavy rainfall, or if the water in the tunnel is more than a couple of inches deep.

Climate
change

Climate change is a problem that adults haven't solved yet. Many still doubt the science and even those that don't aren't perfect role models. In a modern Western world, it is incredibly difficult for most of us (unless blessed with a massive budget) to lead a zero-carbon lifestyle. Given how tricky it is for adults to address, how should we communicate it to children? The fact is that they need to know about climate change if we have any long-term hope of improving the world.

The short-cut way of explaining it is to talk about dying polar bears and melting icecaps. The trouble is, they won't have seen a polar bear in the flesh and the link between your energy usage and the North Pole is very hard to make. Rather than pointing out their more carbon-guzzling activities, it is best to focus on the benefits of taking action.

The key is to help our children care about the world around us. No amount of scientific knowledge and rules about energy wastage will help if, as families, we are not engaged with nature and our environment.

Try to bring climate change discussions into your lives

When turning off the light or hanging clothes on the line: *I'm doing this so we affect the planet less by not wasting electricity.*

Is it better for the environment for us to walk or drive to school? Which should we do today?

We can choose strawberries from Egypt or apples from down the road. Which have used less energy, or less carbon, to get to us?

We're going on holiday to Spain – would you help me offset our flights online? This helps to make up for the carbon we will use to get there.

What could we do differently to use less carbon?

Talk about landscapes and how they change over time. How does climate change affect hills, mountains, and coastlines?

Discuss the difference between natural change (such as seasons) and change brought about by humans.

Ask them what the difference is between the weather and the climate.

A young phenologist hard at work

Phenology

Phenology is the study of seasonal natural phenomena, especially in relation to the climate, and plant and animal life. It is a lovely way of connecting children with nature and considering the impacts of weather and climate on species.

It's really easy to do – just give them a notepad to record their first sighting of:

- snowdrops
- a bee
- frogspawn
- a butterfly
- a swallow
- a ladybird.

Each year you'll be able to compare previous entries and it will make spring even more exciting. It can also be a good trigger for talking about climate versus weather. Short-term weather changes can affect these natural events, but it is the longer-term patterns over many years that are influenced by climate change.

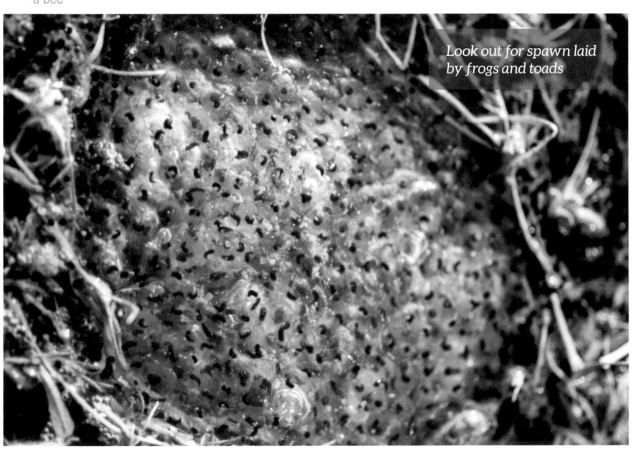

Look out for spawn laid by frogs and toads

Your child may not remember to do this year after year, but you can compare just one entry with online examples from around the country, or with historical records. Try the Woodland Trust Nature's Calendar for other people's sightings.

Amazing educational **activities**

Some activities are pure play magic. They will entrance children, challenge bodies and minds, as well as teaching kids masses about the world around them.

Relight my fire

Hypnotic, dangerous and compelling, lighting a fire is one of the most exciting things you can do with children (best for those over the age of three). Many people believe children and fire should be kept well apart, but learning fire safety is actually one of those life skills such as swimming and road safety, which, once you know the rules, can make you safer in the long run.

Just as you wouldn't put a non-swimmer in a fast-flowing river for their first dip, make sure your first fire together is e small, contained and manageable.

You will need:

- a place where fires are allowed, such as your garden, certain campsites or local woodland with the landowner's permission
- matches
- firelighter (for beginners and guaranteed success)
- dry sticks of various sizes – roughly a carrier bagful for a good starter fire
- a sheet or two of newspaper or other scrap paper, scrunched up

Learn how to enjoy a campfire safely

- marshmallows (find long thin sticks to toast them)
- a shovel
- a large container of water (for extinguishing the fire, but keep some spare in case of a burn).

First, choose your site. Make sure you are at least five metres from tents, shrubs or anything flammable. Use your shovel to clear an area of ground roughly a metre squared of sticks and debris – aim for bare ground or green grass (no dead grass). Dig a smaller indentation in the centre of your clearing, about the size of a large dinner plate – this is your firepit.

Place the scrunched-up paper and firelighter (if using) in your firepit, then arrange the sticks in a wigwam-style pyramid around. Make sure the tiniest sticks are on the inside next to the paper.

Use a match or two to light the paper or firelighter from two sides (adults only). Give it a blow if there is no wind and it is looking reluctant.

Keep topped up with bigger sticks once it is established. Pop a marshmallow on a long thin stick and toast it – beware, they are very hot (but so delicious) when toasted!

To extinguish your fire, let it die down to the embers then pour over the water. Use the shovel to stir the wet, ashy mixture until you are satisfied the embers are cool.

There are no rules against bonfires in your garden or backyard but you could be fined if you allow the smoke to drift across the road and become a danger to traffic. This is unlikely with a tiny fire but do check the wind's direction first.

No campfire is complete without toasted marshmallows

Green [CHALLENGE] #3

Teach your daughter how to wee outside! This is an essential skill for days spent in the countryside where toilets are not so accessible. It is easier for boys but takes a bit more mastering for girls, so let them practise and make sure you have a change of clothes available.

A word of advice: make sure both boys and girls know where is suitable for al-fresco weeing – no one welcomes a kid who urinates next to their tent.

Fire rules and safety

- No running near fires.
- Careful supervision of the fire, children and any pets by adults at all times.
- Don't put anything other than sticks on the fire. Plastic causes noxious fumes and can be dangerous when melted, and aerosols or batteries can explode.
- Think about clothing – check that coats and other garments are flame-resistant and avoid synthetics that can melt onto the skin if a spark lands on them.
- Keep firelighters and matches out of reach of children.
- If anyone gets burnt, cool the burn with lukewarm or cool (not iced) water and cover with clingfilm. Seek medical advice quickly.

Beware the woodland creatures!

Den building

Childhood is not complete without regular den building. Indoors with sheets and chairs is fine for soggy days, but for the real deal you've got to get outside.

You will need an area with trees and long sticks, string and a penknife or scissors (not essential but can help for more complicated den structures, such as the wigwam!).

Basic tent-style den

Find a strong-looking Y-shaped tree and lean the longest stick you can find in the Y, with the other end wedged into the ground. Now prop other sticks on to this frame to form a wall on each side. Build on to these walls until few gaps remain (except your door!). Next, cover your structure with dead leaves or ferns to block out the light and provide shelter from the wind.

Finally, you need to find some logs for seats and decide on your secret password for entry.

Wigwam den

Wigwam dens are great because they are free-standing. You will need to find several long, sturdy branches to lean against each other to make the main frame. Tying them together with string can help make this extra secure.

Now prop other branches around this structure and don't forget to leave a door. Cover with dead leaves or ferns for more shelter.

Teddy den

Younger children can be kept away from all that stick-swinging action by building a smaller teddy-sized den. Propping sticks against a log or smaller tree will make a cosy nook for a favourite teddy and create some lovely storytelling opportunities.

A basic tent den coming along nicely

Den rules and safety

- Grown-ups are only allowed in dens if express permission has been granted and they know the secret password (or have chocolate).

- Do not prop large or heavy logs above head height.

- Only use dead sticks – don't damage living shrubs or trees to make your den.

- Wear long trousers to protect your skin from insects – especially important if you are in an area where there may be ticks or leeches.

Urban **jungle**

If you live in a busy city with little access to the countryside, finding wholesome natural activities for your children can seem challenging. In fact, there are many opportunities for a green life. There are likely to be more options for public transport and walking is often safer – rural roads sometimes lack pavements.

Urban parks can offer amazing spaces. Make the most of the playground and then head for a patch of open grass to look for mini-beasts.

Botanical gardens can be a lovely place to escape the hubbub and enjoy the colours and scents of different plants.

The banks of city rivers are great for a stroll, and offer a good chance to spot wildlife, such as kingfishers and summertime dragonflies, even in the centre of London. Seals have been spotted in the Thames and the Thames Estuary, for example, is full of wading birds.

Inheritance

Parents and schools undoubtedly play a massive role in their children's education, but don't forget the older generation.

Intergenerational learning can be the greatest gift a grandparent can give. Many grandparents can feel second-best when compared with technology and whizzy play parks, but they are likely to have grown up with more freedom to roam than today's children, so can help introduce some wild adventure back into youngsters' lives. They may also have more practical experience with traditional cooking and gardening than parents.

Wildlife clubs such as those organized by the RSPB or Wildlife Trusts can also bring opportunities to meet inspirational volunteers of all ages to spark a lifetime of interest in nature. I loved hearing that the young Wildlife Explorers I met when I worked at the RSPB are now studying zoology and environmental sciences at university.

On-the-job learning

Is it Green or Gross...

to let your pre-schooler eat soil?

Virtual parenting

As a mother, I give a thousand thanks a day for how much I can achieve from the confines of my house. Virginia Woolf famously wrote that a woman needs "a room of one's own" in order to work, explore her creativity, seek independence and fulfil her potential. Now the modern equivalent is surely an iPhone of one's own.

The web is abuzz with working parents, many of them mothers based at home or staying on top of the workload while on the school run. But what of our children? How often have you noticed parents obliviously twiddling away on their phones while Jemima whacks another child or tries to seek parental approval for her magnificent see-sawing? Once I was so absorbed in checking my emails that I failed to notice my children had covered themselves in my lipstick metres away. Of course, we reason, our children should understand that they are not the sole purpose for our existence. What a great role model we are by being at the park yet still taking that important call! Surely it's better than not being there at all?

Social media is always present. I'll even confess to a mild addiction. It's that #fearofmissingout that does it. And goodness, who isn't grateful for a little respite from the wonderful tedium of childcare? A reminder that you are still part of the world can certainly help to keep the insanity at bay.

However, social media is a slippery slope. I read a tweet recently: "I am in bed with my kids reading their favourite story. Utter joy." Well, no: you are failing to fully focus on the utter joy of your children. We seem to require constant stimulation from the virtual world, and it can lead to our children grabbing any opportunity to get their grubby little paws on our technology 'toys'. When I first had a mobile phone, I used to turn it off between calls. Now turning it off is the very last thing I do before I turn out the light.

I want to be present in the moment. I want to hear what my children say the first time they say it. I want to have a clearer line between work and play. I want to reduce my energy use. How about you?

Green [CHALLENGE] #4

Try a whole week without using your smartphone or tablet in front of the children.

Escape technology by getting outdoors – after all, you don't want to drop your phone in the stream

Put technology in its place

Five years ago, few parents would have allowed a child under 12 their own phone, but now it is not unusual for primary-school children to inherit their parents' old smartphones.

Boundaries are shifting and you will have to draw your own lines in the sand, ones that fit your values without turning your child into someone from the sixteenth century in the eyes of their friends.

Sensible rules for technology

- Don't let your kids use anything that you can't – keep up or you'll lose control.

- Don't allow your kids to bully you into buying them a device that is purely for status – will they really use it?

- Check your safe browsing is activated on all devices in your home.

- Balance screen time with outdoors time.

- No televisions in bedrooms.

- Mobiles off at night and not at the dinner table.

- Don't forget technology can be amazing and help you discover the world. See Chapter 7 for information on how technology can help you explore nature.

Footnotes for Chapter 1

1 Whitebread, D. et al. (2012). 'The importance of play'.
http://www.importanceofplay.eu/IMG/pdf/dr_david_whitebread_-_the_importance_of_play.pdf

2 Bellinger, D. C. (2012). 'Chemical exposures cause child IQ losses that rival major diseases'.
http://www.environmentalhealthnews.org/ehs/newscience/2012/01/2012-0223-chemicals-iq-loss-similar-to-disease

3 Faber Taylor, A. et al. (2011). 'Could exposure to everyday green spaces help treat ADHD?
Evidence from children's play settings'. *Applied Psychology: Health and Well-Being* 3: 281-303.

4 Blakesley, D. et al. (2013). 'Engaging children on the autistic spectrum with the natural environment: Teacher insight study and evidence review'. Natural England Commissioned Reports, NECR116.http://publications.naturalengland.org.uk/publication/11085017

5 Gardner, B. (2011). 'The joys of learning outside the classroom'. *Special Educational Needs*.
https://www.senmagazine.co.uk/articles/articles/senarticles/the-joys-of-learning-outside-the-classroom

6 Hope, C. (2013). 'One school playing field sold off every three weeks since Coalition was formed'.
http://www.telegraph.co.uk/education/keep-the-flame-alive/10516870/One-school-playing-field-sold-off-every-three-weeks-since-Coalition-was-formed.html

7 Living Streets and Parentline Plus (2014). 'Living Streets and Parentline Plus walk to school report'.
http://www.livingstreets.org.uk/sites/default/files/content/library/Reports/Living%20Streets%20and%20Parentline%20Plus%20Walk%20to%20School%20report.pdf

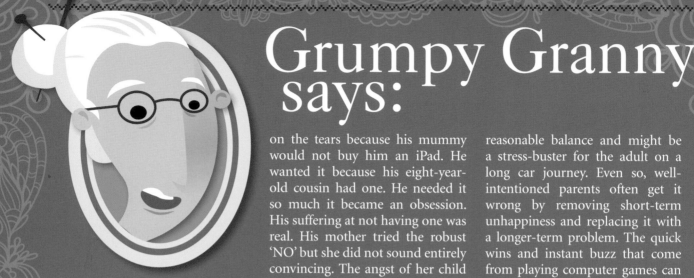

Grumpy Granny says:

Nothing ventured

Full of opinions, frequently right, Grumpy Granny thinks you could be raising your children in a better way. As mother of four children and a grandmother of seven, she has plenty of experience to draw on, as well as the older generation's perspective on our modern, less-than-eco-friendly ways.

Children place a higher value on something they don't have. Parents would do well to remember that when they mollycoddle their children, giving them whatever they want and showering them with all manner of material goods from smartphones to designer clothes. When kids pester for stuff, it is the adult's job to say no – and mean it. My grandchild, at five, turned on the tears because his mummy would not buy him an iPad. He wanted it because his eight-year-old cousin had one. He needed it so much it became an obsession. His suffering at not having one was real. His mother tried the robust 'NO' but she did not sound entirely convincing. The angst of her child was genuine and she wanted to remove his pain.

Some digital is OK. Playing on an adult's tablet or smartphone, with control and ownership remaining strictly with the adult, can give a

Taking a calculated risk

reasonable balance and might be a stress-buster for the adult on a long car journey. Even so, well-intentioned parents often get it wrong by removing short-term unhappiness and replacing it with a longer-term problem. The quick wins and instant buzz that come from playing computer games can make the slow-burn rewards from exploring the real world difficult and unappealing.

Bringing up kids is all a risk game. The risk of physical danger is an essential part of living life to the full, and a life without challenge can lead to a bored child more vulnerable to stress. The difficulty for a parent is deciding how much risk to allow and how to avoid feeling guilty when a child is hurt. Outdoor freedom can result in cuts and grazes, stings and even broken bones; but climbing trees, riding bikes, making dens, lighting fires and damming streams bring excitement and pleasure. Bad things may happen but children will learn to take more care in future. Given the chance, they will develop the skills they need to keep themselves safe. This will be a firm foundation for growing up.

Your green nest

How will you make your home sustainable and natural?

2

Our home should be our nest: cosy, safe and with just enough room for our fledglings to practise stretching their wings – without breaking the lamp.

In practice, many of our homes are rammed full of toys and possessions, loads of which we no longer use. And if your home is like mine, there are probably also slug stripes of wiped snot on the sofa and smeared fingerprints on door frames as well as the world's biggest pile of laundry.

On top of all this, the average home is filled with many different types of chemicals that society has conditioned us to believe are necessary for hygiene purposes. In my own cupboard I once counted 22 different bottles of cleaning stuff. You'd think my home would be sparkling!

I've read many an article that makes me feel paranoid about toxins and deadly chemicals in household products. Many parents blame them for causing or exacerbating conditions such as eczema or asthma. It's easy to become fearful, but a little knowledge can help you work out what you need to avoid. Firstly, there is no such thing as 'chemical-free' (whatever your shampoo or eco-cleaner says on the label). All matter contains molecules that are made through chemical reactions; even water is a chemical.

The trick is to work out which chemicals are good and which are harmful. It's not as easy as working out which chemicals are natural and which are man-made. For example, would you prefer a dose of organically grown belladonna or manufactured sodium hydrogen carbonate? I'd choose the latter – harmless bicarbonate of soda – over the natural but oh-so-deadly plant.

We have been trained by marketeers to believe that we need to use many different products around the home to eradicate all germs. This can feel especially pertinent when we have little ones crawling around putting everything in their mouths. Actually the removal of all bacteria may not be in our children's interests – I strongly believe in a little immune-raising dirt and when every surface is sterilized, this simply won't happen.

Certainly reducing our use of petroleum-based chemicals (this can include types of soap, solvents, detergents, paints and many more) is good for the planet and our wallets. Luckily there are lots of effective, safe, natural alternatives.

Your home is also where a great deal of your energy use happens. You may have been quite frugal until your kids arrived, but suddenly their needs come first. Before, a low thermostat and lots of jumpers felt fine, but the fear of chilly babes in their beds has most of us leaping for the heating switch. Now the guilty rumble of the tumble dryer may be the musical accompaniment to your Sunday evenings when you realize you've forgotten to hang the school uniform out on the line.

With all that cleaning, washing, drying, cooking and keeping the place warm, it is likely that your family's carbon footprint will grow even faster than a two-year-old's tootsies.

There is another way though. Just a few simple changes can make a massive difference to your impact on the environment. Not only that, but it will result in a healthier, more inspiring place to live for all of you.

Recycled cleaning cloths and brushes are a good start

The big green
clean

I dream of a beautiful home: all calming creams and natural neutrals. The big sash windows would be open, letting a summer's breeze gently billow my fine white curtains and bringing the scent of wisteria into my garden room. That's plan A and it's not going to happen for various reasons, not least my failure to win the lottery.

However, I can achieve plan B – a welcoming, lived-in home that is naturally cleaned and provides a healthy place for my children to grow up in while being sensitive to their planet. The first thing to do is to look at the products you are using. Invest in some natural but powerful ingredients that every super cleaner needs:

- white vinegar
- bicarbonate of soda
- beeswax
- tea-tree oil
- soapnut shells.

Diluted in water, plain white vinegar will sort those bleary windows and used neat in the loo overnight with a bit of a scrub, it will also tackle limescale.

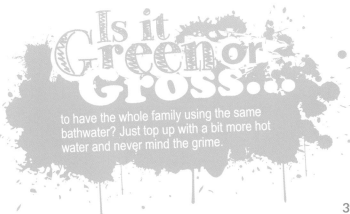

Is it Green or Gross...

to have the whole family using the same bathwater? Just top up with a bit more hot water and never mind the grime.

Bicarbonate of soda is brilliant for cleaning the oven. Just sprinkle it in the bottom and add a good old splosh of vinegar. Watch it fizz (this is a good spectator sport for children at an eye-safe distance) then simply wipe it down an hour later.

Beeswax is fabulous for wooden furniture and floors and is so much better for the environment than using aerosol sprays full of artificial scents.

Tea-tree oil is a powerful antifungal and antibacterial agent. A mixture of tea-tree oil and water (in an empty spray bottle) makes an excellent all-purpose cleaner around the home (just fill the bottle with water and add two teaspoons of tea-tree oil).

A mixture of apple-cider vinegar with a few drops of tea-tree oil scrubbed on to mould will keep your bathroom sparkling. A sprinkle of tea-tree oil in pets' bedding will help deter fleas, and a drip or two in the nappy bucket will keep it smelling fresh.

Soapnut shells are amazing for washing your laundry. Soapnuts come from the soapberry tree and their shells produce natural soap, which is organic and sustainable. The shells are brown and wrinkled and look a bit like dried dates. Simply pop a few in a muslin bag (usually provided) with your dirty laundry to replace detergents and fabric conditioners in your washing machine. They are totally natural, organic, and paraben, phosphate, petrochemical and toxin free which makes them good for sensitive skin (and safe for marine life). Even better, after you have used them for four or five washes, you just compost them.

It takes a bit of time to get used to seeing your washing machine going round with no bubbles, but that is because there are no foaming agents – bubbles don't clean. Your clothes will smell neutral and fresh, but not perfumed, and will feel reasonably soft. Most importantly, they will be clean. Even cloth nappies.

You can also cook soapnut shells in water to produce a soapy liquid that is good for all sorts of cleaning. Look online for many ideas on how to use them in shampoo, dishwashers, for athlete's foot treatments and more.

Use soapnut shells for eco-clean laundry

Happy **workers**

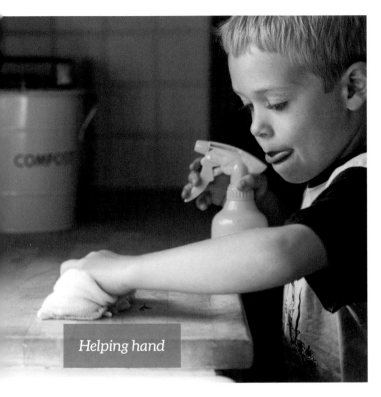

Helping hand

I'm all for a little child labour if it gets my home clean – from my own children, that is. Young children can learn to love cleaning and older ones can carry out additional tasks to earn a few pounds. Try filling a spray bottle with water and a few drops of essential oils so your child can spray and wipe kitchen cupboards.

Have a teddy bath time using soapnut shells, a few drops of lavender oil and teddies piled into the sink or bath then cuddled in towels and hung on the line to drip-dry.

Urban **jungle**

If you live in a city, you are less likely to have a garden, so your indoor space may have to double up as a place for your little ones to let off steam as well as hide away from the world.

However small your home, try and make sure your child has:

- a private place to play where they can retreat for some quiet time, such as a den area in the corner of the lounge, or an area that is just theirs in a shared bedroom. You could paint the individual sections of a shared bedroom different colours to give each child a sense of their own identity and space;
- a communal place to play without getting in the way or being told off constantly for leaving toys out;
- ideally, a chance to flow between private and communal spaces freely, although little ones will need help with stairs.

Green [CHALLENGE] #5

Step away from the kitchen roll for a whole week. Although it's great for occasional spills (I'd go insane in my kitchen if I denied myself this), if you use it for everyday cleaning you are wasting resources. A reusable cloth, flannel or old clothes cut into rags is the green alternative.

When you do use kitchen roll, compost it afterwards. It will biodegrade quickly with grass clippings and veg peelings and will improve the quality of your compost.

Purify your air with plants

Many of us know that rainforests and trees work hard for us, transforming carbon dioxide into oxygen, providing shelter and purifying our air. So why do we often overlook the role plants can play in our homes, particularly in children's bedrooms?

NASA, no less, has researched the best plants to filter air, so they can select what to grow in a space station.[1] As well as producing oxygen, the following plants will also absorb pollutants such as the delightful benzene, formaldehyde and trichloroethylene, which may be released by many common household items, such as hair or nail products, plastic dishes, non-iron clothing, glues or cleaning products. These plants are all easy to grow indoors and inexpensive, especially if you buy them when small. The average home should ideally contain a plant in every room in order to improve the air quality.

>> **Top 5** plants to ... purify the air in a family home

1. Spider plant
2. Gerbera daisy
3. Rubber plant
4. Bamboo palm
5. Weeping fig

Other plants such as English ivy and the peace lily are excellent air purifiers but can be toxic if eaten by humans or pets, so place these well out of reach.

A forest grew

A lovely project that brings plants into your home is the creation of a miniature garden or forest, known as a terrarium – that's the plant equivalent of an aquarium. Your plants will live inside a glass container, a magical ecosystem that even has its own climate (the air inside the container is likely to be warmer).

To make your own gorgeous terrarium, first decide if you would like a moist or dry environment – choose dry if you think remembering to water it may be an issue.

You will need about four or five individual plants (depending on the size of your container). The miniature varieties are best.

A terrarium – the whole world in your hands

Dry terrarium

Choose an open glass container such as a goldfish bowl, vase or deep glass casserole dish. Suitable plants include succulents and cacti.

Moist terrarium

Choose a glass container with a lid such as a cookie jar, lidded aquarium or large mason jar. Suitable plants include ferns, ivies, begonias and moss.

Once you have selected your container and plants, you will need:

- gravel
- activated charcoal (this is optional but will help filter the water; you can buy it from the aquarium section of a pet store)
- potting soil
- small rocks and pebbles, the more decorative the better.

Place a layer of gravel about 3cm (1") deep at the bottom of your container. This will provide drainage for your plants. Next, add 1cm (½") of charcoal (if using) and then your potting soil up to half full. Lightly pat it down and insert your plants, making sure they are well fixed in place.

Add in a few decorative rocks and anything else that takes your fancy, such as pine cones, Lego mini-figures, plastic insects or fairies to make it an interesting little world.

Place your terrarium somewhere reasonably light, but not in direct sunlight. If you've chosen succulents and cacti, water once or twice a month; but water or spray ferns weekly.

Wildlife in **your home**

We all live with lots of tiny creatures in our homes. Some of these, such as flies and dust mites, are of course unwelcome, but we also house all sorts of interesting and harmless creatures that are fun to explore with children.

Silverfish

These rather attractive metallic-sheened insects are considered a pest, as they eat books and cotton. Mainly, though, they like dead skin cells! I have never seen them as a problem, although a massive infestation wouldn't be good. As ever, moderation is the key.

Silverfish can live a whole year without eating. They are nocturnal and preyed on by house spiders. If your children want to find out if you have them in your home, set a harmless trap overnight. Wrap an empty glass jar with masking tape, leaving the hole exposed. Pop a little bread inside and leave the jar out overnight (in the kitchen is a good bet). The silverfish will be able to climb in on the tape, but will be unable to escape.

Spiders

Some of you just won't be able to tolerate the thought of being kind to spiders when they are the most terrifying creatures alive … maybe. But I would urge you to try and avoid passing your phobias on. House spiders can be fascinating to children. You can even learn to identify male and female spiders because the males have longer legs and the females have broader abdomens. They can be very useful, keeping flies and other insects under control. They are most easily found in dark, forgotten corners, such as the back of a cupboard or behind the radiator. The shed or a log pile is a good bet too. Catch them gently with your hand and place in a jar with a few holes in the lid. If you want to keep a spider as a pet, you just need to feed it live insects such as flies a few times a week. Watching them hunt is amazing.

Also look out for the creatures known as 'daddy-long-legs', which are likely to be either crane flies (slender flies with erratic flight) or harvestmen (skinny spider lookalikes most often found in corners at ceiling height).

Nesting birds

Swallows and other species, such as starlings and house martins, used to regularly nest in the eaves of old houses. Modern buildings and the renovation of older properties leaves them no place to nest. You can address that by putting up nest boxes on your home – read more about how to do this in Chapter 6. We have swallows above my son's room. He loves listening to the parents bringing food for the noisy youngsters in springtime.

If you do find that birds are nesting in your eaves, remember it is illegal to disturb them.

Bats

As their natural habitats have been lost, bats have adapted to roost in houses. Halloween has given bats a bad reputation as spooky and scary. Actually, they are very beautiful creatures and if you are lucky enough to have bats in your attic, it's no big deal. They aren't rodents so won't nibble your wires or wood like a mouse would. Bats don't build nests, so they aren't bringing messy bedding material into your home. Their droppings crumble away to dust and there are no known health risks associated with bat poo. Unlike mice or rats, you won't get infested with bats because a female bat usually only has one baby a year.

On top of that, most bats eat insects so they are helping to control pests. It's time to go batty for bats!

Sharing our home with these beautiful swallows

Your child's
bedroom

As the venue for all that sweet baby sleep (hopefully), your child's bedroom needs to be calming as well as having character for daytime play.

Forget all the gender-based pirates and princesses rubbish. For inspiration, you need look no further than outside your window. Nature-themed bedrooms can be relaxing and educational. They can also be suitable for longer, unlike a passing brand-related obsession that may be over within weeks.

Nature art in your child's bedroom can inspire

Create a natural bedroom for your child

Choose natural wall colours, such as sand, blues, greens or taupe, which create a peaceful neutral backdrop they won't quickly outgrow. It is worth paying a little more for eco-paints, which will be low in fumes and better for the environment. Standard paint production involves the use of non-sustainable petrochemical-based resources. Making just 1 litre of paint can result in up to 30 litres of toxic waste, and if paint is disposed of incorrectly it will pollute waterways and damage habitats.

Natural fibres for your carpets are a good choice because they are not petrochemical-based and will biodegrade when no longer wanted. Consider wool or sisal. Check if your old carpet can be recycled: the dealer of your new carpet may take it, or look for local carpet-recycling schemes. It could be made into a new carpet or even a fishing net.

If you are a new parent you'll need more storage than you ever thought possible! Try seagrass or wicker for renewable and attractive alternatives to plastic.

Next, introduce colour and character with wall stickers or art inspired by woodland creatures, marine life or flowers and mini-beasts. A stunning picture or photo of nature or wildlife could make a brilliant present for a new baby – something they will treasure for life.

Bring in natural materials too – for example, how about a real branch (carefully secured and out of reach of little paws) complete with a (cuddly) owl perched on it?

Eco-friendly
clothing

Clothes matter. They are how we present ourselves to the world and how we want to be perceived. It's a sad fact that if your child is having a screaming fit in the supermarket, you are more likely to gain sympathetic looks if your noisy rascal is dressed head to toe in Boden than if they look like they have just emerged from the woods, complete with grass stains, wild hair and a stick sword.

Many people get sucked in to trying to dress their children like catalogue models, but we need to dress our kids for action, not looks. The way forward is durable clothes that facilitate movement. A child becoming too focused on their appearance at an early age is not a recipe for a balanced life.

What about the environmental impacts of our clothing choices?

Before you buy

- Look for clothes made in your country – this is surprisingly hard to achieve but buying UK-produced items means you are avoiding sweatshops or child labour.
- See if you can buy secondhand instead.

You'll need plenty of storage, so choose natural alternatives to plastic

- Pass your children's outgrown clothes on to friends – believe in the great wheel of sharing and hopefully plenty will come your way when you need it.
- Buy a season ahead for the best deals, particularly on auction websites – for example, shorts will be cheaper in winter.

Hand-knitted clothes look super-cute as well as being environmentally sound. Try merino or cashmere if normal wool is too itchy. Consider organic especially for cotton, which is by far the most used fabric in the world. It is usually grown using liberal amounts of pesticides, herbicides and synthetic fertilizer and an estimated one quarter of all the agricultural insecticides applied globally each year.[2] It makes sense to prioritize organic for clothes next to the skin, such as pyjamas, underwear and bedding.

When you've bought

Make sure the kids actually wear the clothes they have – saving items for best can mean they are only worn once or twice. What's wrong with party dresses for the park (with jeans underneath)?

Recycle. If they are too worn, use as rags for dusting or making dolls' clothes. Alternatively, find the nearest fabric recycling drop-off point.

Is it Green or Gross...

to spot-wash clothes to get an extra day of wear from them? Just rub off that bit of yoghurt!

Get knitting or go organic

Why the colour of your children's clothes is an environmental issue

From the very moment you give birth, a sea of gender-specific colour floods into your home.

This colour-coding may be handy for androgynous-looking babies, but why should clothes for girl crawlers, toddlers, climbers and walkers be so different? Even a simple T-shirt will often be made in a thinner material and it is harder to find durable trousers for girls. Do girls spend less time mucking around outside than boys? Of course not, but leggings or capri pants won't always provide the warmth or knee protection required. Girls' shorts are often designed to be a few inches shorter than boys' versions, failing to protect their legs from the sun.

School uniform reinforces gender stereotypes. Girls' polo shirts will have more detail on the collar, and girls will often be expected to wear skirts or pinafores. Why should our girls wear these to play hopscotch in a cold winter playground? It seems that the world is determined to send girls the message that they are here to look pretty. Meanwhile, our boys' typical clothes often feature action superheroes. Do we really want them to look tough and act tougher?

I kept most of my son's basic clothes to reuse, but to my eyes some of them just looked funny on my younger daughter. Despite my best intentions, I had been conditioned to see my little girl in a certain way. I also wanted her to look like her friends, and no one else I knew seemed to dress their daughter in boys' clothes. Did it mean I had to put my hand in my pocket and buy a whole new wardrobe for her?

We have become victims of marketing. Shops encourage gender difference because it forces us to buy twice. This wastes our money and the planet's resources. Luckily there is another way. It is possible for our kids to look yummy-scrummy and feel comfy without sacrificing too much cash and natural resources. So here are my top tips on rule-free dressing:

Catch a rainbow

Buy carefully in the first place. There is no point in buying flimsy clothes, which often come with considerable air miles and are more likely to disintegrate in the wash within weeks. Instead look for good-quality organic cottons which will last well and avoid chemical residues. Even if you don't plan to have any more children, the hand-me-on options are doubled for colours such as red and yellow.

Have a go at customizing clothes – you may surprise yourself

Top 10 ways to ... have an eco-friendly school uniform

1. For shirts and polo shirts, buy Fairtrade organic cotton.

2. Avoid scalloped collars on polo shirts (thus keeping them gender-neutral so they can be handed on to a boy or a girl).

3. Avoid uniform that has been treated with non-iron and stain-repelling chemicals such as Teflon or formaldehyde.

4. Buy secondhand – this is particularly good for pinafores, summer dresses and shorts, which get less wear.

5. Line-dry white polo shirts and shirts to naturally keep them bright, but make sure you line-dry coloured sweaters inside out to minimize premature fading.

6. Seek out eco-friendly leather shoes which have been coloured using non-toxic dyes and are solvent-free.

7. Ask your school if they would set up a uniform exchange scheme, or have a stall at the end-of-year cake sale or school fair, where secondhand uniform is donated and resold.

8. Buy a size larger than you need – you'll be surprised how soon it fits perfectly and this allows for a little fabric shrinkage too.

9. Mend any tears, and consider cutting off and hemming old trousers to make school shorts (if you can't / won't sew, then try iron-on hems).

10. Label uniforms with just your family name and landline number to avoid relabelling for siblings.

Customize

You don't need to be a whizz with a sewing machine to have some fun creating original clothes. It's amazing what sewn-on sequins, buttons or a pocket can do to transform a top. Best of all, these can be suited to the child's particular interests, whether that be trains or ponies.

If your daughter is determined to be a princess or fairy, then make or buy her a tiara or wings that can be worn over more practical clothes. Fun superhero capes for either gender will also make the outfit underneath irrelevant – these are easy to make, especially with iron-on hems!

Rebel

Who says boys shouldn't wear tights under their jeans? Why can't your four-year-old daughter wear swimming trunks rather than a frilly one-piece or (even worse) a bikini? There is nothing cooler than boys' jeans with a pretty top on a girl, or a boy in a vibrant yellow and pink T-shirt. Don't be afraid to rewrite the rules, so long as your children are comfortable and happy.

Respect their identity

Environmental concerns are so important, yet we are bringing up an individual with their own view of the world. You should have the final say in their wardrobe, but why not give them a day a week to wear exactly what they want? And don't feel you have to justify their wacky outfit to friends and family – just act like a princess skirt with a fireman's jacket is totally normal.

What about school uniform?

You may feel you have little power to influence the environmental credentials of your child's uniform (see tips left). You can't exactly knit their grey trousers, customize a sweater or be inventive with socks. Nevertheless, there is still room for being top of the class for green, ethical uniforms.

Composting

I love composting to reduce how much kitchen and garden waste goes to landfill

I adore my compost heap. It is so clever the way it takes our veg peelings and all those teabags (do you have any idea how much tea I had to drink in order to write this book?) and turns them into lovely mulchy fertilizer and soil for the garden. The children love it too because it is a ready source of worms, slugs and woodlice to fiddle with – I mean study.

Making a good compost heap is like baking a cake... you need the right blend of wet and dry contents and a magic ingredient (baking powder for your cake, worms for your compost). You also need heat to make the transformation happen – your oven provides this for your cake, but your compost will generate heat itself as it rots down.

Top 10 tips for ...
happy composting

1. If you have space, buy two outside compost bins. This way you can fill one and leave it to rot while filling the other.

2. Pick a level, well-drained site – on soil, not concrete – so the worms can find an easy way in.

3. If you use the compost bin for grass clippings, add some ripped newspaper to stop it going slimy.

4. Don't put cooked food in or you may attract vermin.

5. If it seems very dry, add a little water or even urine.

6. As well as fruit, veg and garden waste, you can add eggshells, teabags and coffee grounds.

7. If you don't have many worms in your compost, dig up a few to get the worm party started. Or buy worms – you can get them by mail order!

8. Give the compost a stir with a stick now and again.

9. Compost is ready to use when it smells clean and earthy and is crumbly and brown in appearance.

10. Spread the finished compost on your flower beds to improve the soil quality, reduce weeds and keep in the moisture.

Is it Green or Gross...

to wee on the compost heap? It saves on water from flushing the loo and the urine can speed up the chemical process involved in making compost. Easier for boys to help with this one!

Urban jungle

Balcony composting

If you don't have a garden, a balcony will do. Just use an old plastic bin or a bucket with a lid. Place dry leaves and a little soil in the bottom and add your fruit and veg peel. Each time you add moist items, add something dry, such as dry leaves or shredded paper. If you can find some worms to add into the mix, so much the better.

Once it is full, give it a stir every week and feel the heat starting to come off it. After several months, you'll have compost ready to add to your tubs and pots. Meanwhile, you can place a potted plant on top of the lid to improve the aesthetics of your compost bin.

For an easier option invest in a compost tumbler, which will fit in a small space and enable you to mix your compost easily (it is a little like a cement mixer in design).

Save energy

There are, of course, the BIG THINGS you can do to save energy around the home, such as cavity wall insulation, installing a more efficient boiler, double-glazing windows and installing solar panels, but there are also many daily actions that don't cost much and can make a big difference.

Top 10 ways to …
save energy in your home

1. Vacuum the dust off the coils behind your fridge (unplug it first) to make it work more efficiently.

2. Descale the kettle to lengthen its life and reduce the electricity needed to make the regular cuppas that every parent deserves.

3. Don't put the oven on until you start food prep – it doesn't need half an hour to get to temperature. You can turn it off five minutes or so before the food is done – it will finish the cooking if you leave the door shut.

4. Share a bath or shower. You'll save water as well as energy if you hop in after, or with, the children.

5. Choose your activities carefully. Do you really have to drive to that trendy music group 12 miles away? Wouldn't the one that is walking distance in the local library do a similar job?

6. Wash full loads only and run the dishwasher when full.

7. Save the tumble dryer for emergencies. An outside clothes line or indoor clothes horse is the way forward 90% of the time.

8. Turn off appliances at the plug when not in use – that includes the baby monitor.

9. Train your children to switch off lights, providing little steps around the house if necessary, and use an energy-efficient nightlight for those nocturnal wanderings.

10. Encourage your children to think about which activities don't require electricity and which do (for example, television versus puzzles).

Invest in an
energy monitor

An energy monitor is a hand-held screen that communicates with your electricity meter to tell you how much electricity you're using in real time. Some can even identify how much electricity individual appliances are using.

They are great for showing children how our actions in the home impact on our energy usage. Set them a challenge to get it as high as possible for one minute and as low as possible for the next.

Is it Green or Gross…

…to save water by not flushing the loo for wee? Will your prissy friend be embarrassed? Will a faint aroma of public loo surround your home?

Green CHALLENGE #6

I'm sure you already recycle bottles and paper, but what about used batteries from all those toys? Just drop them off for recycling when you go to the supermarket and stop all those toxic-heavy metals such as lead and cadmium leaching out of landfill sites.

Footnotes for Chapter 2

1 Wolverton, B. C. et al. (1989). 'A study of interior landscape plants for indoor air pollution abatement'.
   NASA-TM-108061. https://archive.org/stream/nasa_techdoc_19930072988/19930072988_djvu.txt

2 Soil Association (2015). 'Organic cotton'.
   http://www.soilassociation.org/whatisorganic/organictextiles/organiccotton

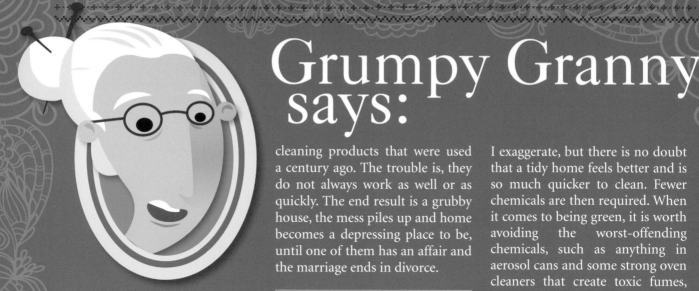

Grumpy Granny says:

Green or sloppy?

Making the home greener can be shorthand for sloppy housekeeping. The younger generation is so stressed and stretched trying to juggle work, childcare, socializing and staying on top of trends that they run out of time. Keeping a clean, tidy home is at the bottom of their list of priorities, unless they have the money to afford a cleaner. (It is beyond me why they would rather have a stranger in the house than do the job themselves.)

Others banish modern chemicals. Out go the things that work quickly and efficiently, eg bleach sprays for cleaning the kitchen and modern detergents for washing clothes, and in come the basic, old-fashioned cleaning products that were used a century ago. The trouble is, they do not always work as well or as quickly. The end result is a grubby house, the mess piles up and home becomes a depressing place to be, until one of them has an affair and the marriage ends in divorce.

Does your home make you feel good?

I exaggerate, but there is no doubt that a tidy home feels better and is so much quicker to clean. Fewer chemicals are then required. When it comes to being green, it is worth avoiding the worst-offending chemicals, such as anything in aerosol cans and some strong oven cleaners that create toxic fumes, but feel free to use other modern cleaning agents and don't feel guilty.

There is a highly effective, green cleaning agent that everyone should use. It is free and effective. It kills germs, removes the environment in which moulds thrive and makes the house smell good. It is easily available but never marketed: fresh air.

I see adults who seem incapable of opening windows unless it is really hot. They do not see the value of removing the damp, germ-ridden air that accumulates in their houses, particularly in the bathroom or the kitchen. Some might turn on the extractor fans, regardless of the energy they use and the noise they make. So remember: you can improve the air quality in your home greenly and for free by simply opening a window.

Can I eat it now?

Eat well and enjoy

3

Like your children's sleep, their eating habits are one of those subjects that has the ability to turn intelligent parents into raving idiots. It is such a primeval desire to see our children eat well that sometimes we forget to trust their instincts.

We try to shovel food into them from an early age under the misguided but compelling belief that the more dinner they eat, the better they will sleep. We cajole them to eat their vegetables and allow them to snack too much in between meals, so we have to do the whole 'just three bites' spoon-feeding routine at the next meal.

Some days they will pick at their food, hardly seeming hungry, or they will hoover up everything in sight and ask for more. This is a sign of a natural appetite in tune with growth and activity, but sometimes we override their needs in order to be satisfied that our children have eaten the 'right' amount. When mealtimes are regularly battlegrounds, it is often easier to provide our children with a less healthy option that we know they will eat than spend a mealtime arguing. No wonder obesity in children is a rising concern.[1]

In the end, we want them to be able to eat a wide range of foods and to make healthy choices for themselves. We want them to understand when they've had enough, but also to enjoy treats and not feel that any foods are outlawed. We want our meals to be happy family times where we can chat, laugh and enjoy our food.

Baby-led weaning (BLW) is ideal for getting the building blocks of healthy eating in place from day one.[2] With BLW, you don't put anything in your child's mouth. They feed themselves from the start of your weaning process. This means sucking, slurping, chewing and even a little gagging. How much food they are actually consuming is anyone's guess, but that is the whole point (control freaks need not apply).

I have tried both methods – the traditional purée-shovelling with my first child and BLW with my second. I am embarrassed to recall the lengths I used to go to encourage my firstborn to eat another spoonful of mush. We'd pop up from under the high chair to make him smile and open his mouth, we'd do aeroplanes, we allowed toys at the table and told stories to distract him, and we'd get so stressed if he didn't want to eat (despite the fact that he was still being breastfed).

The next time around I let my daughter take the lead. BLW is most certainly the messiest experience imaginable. She squelched her food happily, so no need for toys to keep her entertained. She smeared it in her hair, and also got some in her mouth. She tasted lots of flavours off my plate and learnt about different textures. The best bit was that I was free from measuring how much she had consumed. That was up to her and I had to learn to trust her to look after herself.

Several years on and both my children eat pretty well, so I don't believe that how you wean your child influences them for life. In the end, what is right for one child may not work for another. Still, BLW is a good lesson for learning to trust your child's own ability to choose what goes into their body.

We also need to educate our children about food and where it comes from. The supermarket culture means that if your children want strawberries in January, they can have them – but there are often plenty of seasonal alternatives they will enjoy instead.

This chapter is all about how to enjoy food, not feel stressed about it. The more we know about seasonal sustainable ingredients, and the more we involve our children in food decisions, the better for their future and the planet.

Day one – the very first food decision ...
breast or bottle?

Breastfeeding is best for the environment too

So you thought you didn't have to worry about the environmental impacts of how you feed your child until they are six months old and trying solids? Even on day one your milk-feeding choices could come with a considerable carbon footprint. We all know that breast is best for your baby, your figure and your bank balance, but guess what? It's good for the environment too.

Now, breastfeeding is an emotive subject – there are so many mums who desperately wanted to but couldn't. And I'll bet that a worry about their carbon footprint wasn't on their minds when their premature baby wasn't gaining weight or the fifth bout of mastitis hit hard. However, breastfeeding, if you can do it, is the best choice for the planet.

Formula versus boob in purely green terms

Formula feeding	Breastfeeding
Exclusive formula feeding for six months*	Exclusive breastfeeding for six months
• Kettle boiled 910 times	• 500 calories extra daily for mum**
• 35 non-recyclable packs of formula powder	• Reduced menstruation so fewer sanitary products in landfill
• Sterilizer run at least 250 times	***Unless you use it as an excuse to indulge like many of us do, in which case: 700 extra calories daily.* 😊
Not to mention:	
• Processing and distribution	
• Plastic bottles and teats	
• Wasted milk poured down the sink	
• The greenhouse gas methane produced from cows farmed for milk	
*Based on an average of 5 x 210ml (7 fl.oz.) feeds per day, although there will be more frequent smaller feeds at first and less frequent, larger feeds later.	

What if you can't breastfeed your baby?

Sometimes, whether for medical, logistical or emotional reasons, breastfeeding just doesn't work out. If that happens to you, don't beat yourself up. Just a few changes in how you bottle-feed can make a massive difference to the planet.

Top 10 ways to ... reduce the environmental impact of bottle-feeding

1. Use glass baby bottles. Sturdy and often printed with organic ink, these are free from petrochemicals, long-lasting and can be recycled.
2. Recycle formula containers – many councils will accept them in the recycling bin (you may need to remove the plastic rim).
3. Sterilize bottles together rather than just one at a time.
4. Buy formula powders – not the ready-to-drink bottles or cartons – or try goat's milk formula.
5. Learn about your baby's appetite – don't make a full bottle if milk is often wasted.
6. Use a marine-friendly washing-up liquid for cleaning bottles and teats prior to sterilizing.
7. Don't boil more water than you need.
8. Keep your kettle working efficiently by regularly descaling.
9. Feed on demand and enjoy some skin-on-skin time when feeding your baby.
10. Above all, don't stress about it – your child may be the one that saves the world and a little formula milk along the way doesn't matter!

Eat family food, **together**

Children don't need their food processed, shaped like a smiley face and dipped in breadcrumbs. Everyone likes a junky dinner now and again, but don't fall into the trap of thinking that children need different food from adults. Ideally meals will be homemade and eaten as a family as much as possible. I know that's not always easy. When you are working, juggling childcare and after-school clubs, or the children are hungry by 5pm and you're not, it can seem impossible to achieve. Weekends can be a good opportunity to give it a go.

For weeknights, try to make enough for the adult meal so there are leftovers for the children the following day. It doesn't all have to be bland nursery fare. If 'safe' flavours are all they've had, it may take a little while to adjust, but even the younger ones can enjoy mild spices and a variety of different herbs. Why not try roasting those potatoes with rosemary, perk up that chicken with cumin, or make a creamy coconut milk and butternut squash curry, gently spiced with chilli and fragrant with coriander?

If at first you don't succeed, try again ... 10 times. Research has shown that continued exposure to foods a child says they don't like will result in them eating more each time. Usually five to ten times does the trick![3] Humans are programmed to be suspicious of unknown foods, but experience teaches us that they are safe.

Whenever you get the chance, take your meal outside. It is a chance to eat free from the constraints of table manners, and all that fresh air certainly stimulates the appetite.

Family mealtimes aren't always harmonious, but they are important

Is it Green or Gross...

to follow the three-second rule? (Surely if you pick up food off a cleanish floor within three seconds it is still fine to eat?)

Quick ways to prepare home-cooked food

- If you are making a lasagne (which can take a while), make the white sauce stage almost instant by mixing grated Cheddar with a large tub of crème fraîche and a little seasoning.

- If you are making a tomato-based pasta or pizza sauce, make double and freeze half.

- If you are making a sauce, grate the vegetables into it for quicker cooking times and fewer lumps for them to pick out. Or you could liquidize the sauce when it's cooled a little.

It doesn't have to be scorching hot to have a picnic

Where to shop for **your family's food**

I'd like to ban myself from ever going to a supermarket... but that would be idiotic. The supermarket is so helpful for those days when I am stressed and can get a basic trolley dash done in 30 minutes flat. Not to mention the unbeatable convenience of shopping online and delivery to my door, or the times when I suddenly have to buy a present for the birthday party I'd forgotten.

Supermarkets are undeniably successful because they give us what we want at a competitive price when we want it … BUT … alongside their convenience we need to make room for food shopping that is better for our community.

Local bakery, fishmonger and butcher

Use your local independent shops when you can afford to do so. Encourage your children to carry out the ordering and paying, and ask for recipe ideas for meat and fish.

If you live somewhere uber-trendy where the local bakers call themselves artisans and you don't feel you can justify £7.50 for an organic sourdough loaf, let them know! They may have cheaper products available or may need a wake-up call that some people want local organic food as a regular choice, not just for a dinner party show-off special.

>> **Top 10 tips** for ... greening your supermarket shop

1. Stick to seasonal and UK-produced food where possible (check out the seasonal guide pp. 64-65).
2. For imported items, such as chocolate, tea and bananas, look for the Fairtrade symbol.
3. Go organic where you can afford to do so.
4. For meat and eggs, organic is the gold standard, free-range is great, and RSPCA Freedom Food should be your minimum.
5. Avoid overly packaged items and aim for recyclable packaging.
6. When you buy meat for a stew, pie or casserole, buy half the amount that you need and bulk it out with beans or lentils to reduce the carbon footprint.
7. Shop in store rather than online. You'll find it easier to compare items and work out what is seasonal.
8. Buy cupboard supplies in bulk to reduce visits to the supermarket.
9. Don't be seduced by 'buy one, get one free' offers if you won't actually use the extra bag of satsumas.
10. Take your own bags and make sure you reuse and recycle any extra bags you acquire.

Farmers' markets

The colours, the noise, the sometimes inflated prices! Farmers' markets are one of the best ways of teaching your children about local food, seasonality and how to get involved in their own food choices.

Top 10 tips for ... a farmers' market visit

1. Arrive before it gets too busy.
2. Take your own bags.
3. Play 'guess the veg' – your kid should learn the difference between an aubergine and a cauliflower.
4. Ask where vegetables are grown and talk to your children about supporting local farms and the importance of reducing food miles.
5. Give your children a little money each and let them choose the vegetables for their next meal, then involve them in cooking it.
6. Try and buy something new each time.
7. Do ask to taste fruit.
8. Give haggling on price a go.
9. Take cash for easy transactions and to avoid spending more than you planned.
10. When you are home, look online for fabulous recipes for your fresh produce.

Organic veg boxes

These can be a bit kale- and cabbage-heavy for many months of the year, so unless your child is amazing at eating green leafy stuff, have a chat with the supplier and see if a more family-friendly range is available. I find that squashes, potatoes and beetroot will always get eaten, especially when roasted or turned into oven-baked vegetable crisps.

Try stopping at those little roadside stalls and buying some random green beans or free-range eggs. Children find this oddly exciting.

Involve the children in preparing and cooking food

Green #7
[CHALLENGE]

For two weeks, try buying just your basics from the supermarket, and shop around for meat, fish and extras from your local farm shop, independent stores and nearest market. This will help you find out what the alternatives are and how they compare cost-wise. You may be surprised to find some real bargains.

Meat
treat

Even if you are vegetarian, chances are your children may eat some meat and buying local produce is a good way of supporting our nation's farmers.

Meat should be a treat, a once or twice-a-week luxury that enables you to buy the best quality (with highest welfare standards) that you can. According to a study carried out by Oxford University, if we ate red meat no more than three times a week, it would save the NHS £1.2 billion each year.[4] Plus eating less meat can really help combat climate change. UN figures state that rearing cattle puts more greenhouse gases into the atmosphere than transport.[5]

Reducing your meat consumption means that you are likely to reduce your weekly food bill, lose weight and escape a food rut with the discovery of yummy new vegetarian recipes.

Fish for your
dinner

All fish is a good source of protein, and oily fish such as salmon is packed full of brain-boosting omega-3 fatty acids. Fish is a good addition to your family's diet, but how sustainable is it?

Do your bit to stop overfishing

All is not well under the waves. This is because of serious overfishing as well as pressure from climate change and marine pollution.

Put a little fishy on your dishy

Basically, we need to lay off fishing the most threatened species and make sure our fish is farmed or fished sustainably. Ask your fishmonger about seabird-friendly fishing methods … no longlines killing our albatrosses, please! And did you know you should buy fish seasonally? We need to avoid eating them in their breeding seasons to minimize the impact on population size.

Check out this online guide for up-to-date information: www.fishonline.org

Don't forget that there are also many vegetarian sources of omega-3 fatty acids. Milled linseed or whole chia seeds can be sprinkled on cereals or hidden in crumble toppings, bread or baking. Hemp, linseed and rapeseed oils are all packed full of essential fatty acids too and can be used in cooking, baking and salad dressings.

Create a fish wallchart

A simple chart with a red (don't eat) and a green (do eat) section can adorn your kitchen wall. With your children, just draw or print pictures of different fish and place in the relevant section based on the latest guidance and season. Update every month or so and get those fishes to swim to their new places. You could even make the wallchart a world map.

Seasonal fruit and veg guide

Eat with the seasons

Is it Green or Gross…

to eat all parts of the animal? Heart and liver pie anyone?

Green #8 [CHALLENGE]

Do without single-use plastic carrier bags for a month. Did you know that these bags are killing marine life? Creatures such as turtles think the bags are food or get tangled up in them.

We all know that seasonal food is better for the environment. After all, it needs less artificial input, such as heating or pesticides, and it is transported less so has a lower carbon footprint.

Did you know that seasonal food is also better for your health? Fruit and veg picked and eaten in season contain higher levels of nutrients such as vitamin C. Not only that, but food that has travelled a long way will usually cost more. Seasonal food tastes better too. Imported produce is often less fresh and has been picked when under-ripe to give it a longer shelf life for the lengthy journey from field to plate. A good farm shop or farmers' market will stock only locally sourced seasonal produce, so you'll soon get a feel for what to buy and when.

If you are supermarket-bound then try these foods, when they are at their very best. Remember, this is only a guide and the availability of produce is affected by the weather.

January

Carrots, celeriac, celery, garlic, kale, leeks, parsnips, main-crop potatoes, savoy cabbages, swedes, sweet potatoes, turnips, rhubarb.

February

Carrots, celeriac, celery, garlic, kale, leeks, parsnips, main-crop potatoes, savoy cabbages, swedes, sweet potatoes, turnips, rhubarb.

March

Cauliflowers, chives, leeks, parsley, parsnips, purple sprouting broccoli, spring green, cabbages, spring onions, rhubarb, sweet potatoes.

April

Cauliflowers, chives, dill, new potatoes, parsley, peas, rhubarb, rocket, sorrel, spinach, spring onions, watercress.

May

Asparagus, basil, chives, coriander, dill, mint, new potatoes, parsley, peas, radishes, rhubarb, rocket, rosemary, sage, sorrel, spinach, tarragon, thyme, watercress.

June

Asparagus, basil, chives, coriander, dill, mint, new potatoes, parsley, peas, radishes, redcurrants, rhubarb, rocket, rosemary, sage, sorrel, spinach, spring onions, strawberries, tarragon, tomatoes, thyme, watercress.

July

Apricots, aubergines, basil, beans, beetroots, blackcurrants, blueberries, cherries, coriander, courgettes, cucumbers, fennel, garlic, gooseberries, lettuces, mangetout, mint, new potatoes, onions, pak choi, parsley, radishes, raspberries, rocket, rosemary, sage, sorrel, spinach, spring onions, strawberries, tarragon, thyme, tomatoes, watercress.

August

Apricots, aubergines, basil, beans, beetroots, blackcurrants, blueberries, broccoli, cherries, chillies, coriander, courgettes, cucumbers, fennel, figs, garlic, gooseberries, lettuces, main-crop potatoes, mangetout, marrows, mint, onions, oregano, pak choi, parsley, peas, plums, radishes, raspberries, rocket, rosemary, sage, sorrel, spinach, strawberries, sweetcorn, tarragon, thyme, tomatoes, watercress, wild mushrooms.

September

Apples, apricots, artichokes, aubergines, basil, beans, beetroots, blackberries, blueberries, broccoli, butternut squashes, celery, chillies, coriander, courgettes, cucumbers, damsons, fennel, figs, leeks, lettuces, main-crop potatoes, mangetout, marrows, medlar, mint, mushrooms, onions, oregano, parsley, pak choi, parsnips, peas, pears, peppers, plums, rocket, rosemary, sage, sorrel, spinach, strawberries, sweetcorn, thyme, tomato, watercress, wild mushrooms.

October

Apples, artichokes, beetroots, broccoli, butternut squashes, celeriac, celery, chillies, courgettes, fennel, garlic, kale, leeks, medlar, mushrooms, parsnips, pears, pumpkins, quinces, radishes, rocket, sage, shallots, sorrel, sweet chestnuts, sweetcorn, rosemary, wild mushrooms.

November

Apples, artichokes, beetroots, butternut squashes, Brussels sprouts, cauliflowers, celeriac, celery, chard, kale, leeks, main-crop potatoes, parsnips, pumpkins, red cabbages, rosemary, sage, shallots, swedes, sweet chestnuts, sweet potatoes, turnips, wild mushrooms.

December

Beetroots, Brussels sprouts, cauliflowers, celeriac, celery, chard, kale, leeks, main-crop potatoes, parsnips, shallots, swedes, sweet potatoes, turnips, white cabbages.

Of course, we will always end up importing some produce – fruit options in the winter months are limited to rhubarb (or apples that have been stored), so if you don't buy non-UK options you won't find much variety of fruit. The trick is to seek fruit that is in season in southern Europe, rather than flown much further from Africa or America. Hence, buy European citrus fruit in December and January, and imported peaches in July to September. Try to save imported produce from outside Europe (such as bananas, passion fruit and papaya) for a treat.

Don't forget to use your freezer to store seasonal fruit. Cooked apples, pears and rhubarb all freeze well and can be defrosted for a quick compote or crumble filling in the depths of winter. Blackberries and plums can be frozen without pre-cooking.

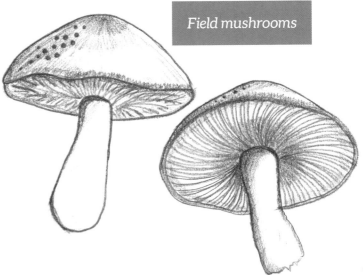

Field mushrooms

It's not just about your fruit and vegetables ...

Try replacing imported pasta and rice with cereals grown in the UK. Spelt, barley and oats are nutritious and stabilize blood glucose levels. Spelt and pesto risotto is a good family fill-up; barley is lovely in a warming soup or stew; and oats are brilliant in baking and in crumble toppings, including savoury toppings.

Swap imported olive oil for locally produced rapeseed oil. It has high levels of monounsaturated fatty acids like olive oil but is even lower in saturated fat and has higher levels of healthy omega-3s. You can use it in baking too.

Top 5 cakes to ... make with vegetables

1. Courgette and chocolate cake
2. Beetroot and chocolate brownies
3. Spiced carrot and raisin muffins
4. Sweet potato and white chocolate cupcakes
5. Parsnip and maple syrup cake

Courgette and chocolate cake – a guaranteed kiddie-pleaser

Green #9 [CHALLENGE]

Have a go at seasonal Sundays, a day of the week when everything you eat is seasonal and locally sourced.

Is it Green or Gross...

to eat things past their sell-by date? Do you bin, or sniff and see?

Simple, fresh, seasonal food doesn't need much packaging

Cut the
waste!

When you are footloose and kiddie-free, avoiding food waste isn't too challenging if you try. You buy a basket of items that fit nicely into your small fridge. You cook what you want and clear your plate. Job done.

Chuck some small people into the mix and suddenly you shop in bulk and you need a fridge the size of a house where things quickly get lost, forgotten and slimy. Not only that, but the young tyrants will randomly refuse to eat a whole plateful of lovingly prepared food. You feel guilty sending them to school with a just-out-of-date yoghurt and end up binning it.

In fact, as much as half of all the food produced in the world (equivalent to a mind-blowing two billion tonnes) ends up as waste every year.[6] Food waste in the home costs the average household with children approximately £700 per year[7] – just think what you could have done with that money instead! To put it into perspective, if we stopped wasting this food it would have the same impact on the environment as removing one in four cars off the road.

We can grumble about supermarkets seducing us into buying more than we need with 'buy one, get one free' deals, or feel hard done by that the children never eat all their vegetables, but this is one green issue which lies firmly within our control. The trick is to plan your meals and be ruthless when you shop. Then stack your fridge in date order. This is highly dull, oh yes, but there is nothing more needlessly wasteful than eating the newest yoghurts while the almost-out-of-date ones cry silently in the icy depths.

The internet enables us to find recipes based on the random ingredients we have available. With fridges, freezers, blenders and ovens, we really are equipped to avoid food waste.

Farm
stories

Old MacDonald had a ... vital learning experience to offer ... eee-i-eee-i-o

Marketeers have long understood the appeal of the farm to young children and their parents. Just look at the amount of farm animals and tractors that appear on toys, puzzles, books and even kids' crockery, jumpers and bedding.

Make sure your children see real farming

At a very young age babies learn that cows go moo and sheep go baa – and this includes kids brought up in cities who've never seen a farm animal in the flesh. The reality is that farming is remote from the lives of most parents and their children. What is really being experienced is the 'cute-ification' of farming. Despite the cuddly sheep on their beds, a generation of children are growing up removed from the reality of food production. Adults can be reluctant to explain that beef is cow, or that the lamb in their story book is the source of the Sunday roast.

Farm animals may be seen in the zoo-like conditions of the petting farm, or through a car window as little dots on the horizon. The gap between fact and fiction has grown as the scale and industrialization of agriculture has increased. Farms are busy and potentially dangerous. Getting up close to farm animals can be risky, whether we are talking about E. coli or an over-excited young heifer.

Over the last 10 years, 31 children aged under 16 have been killed on farms[8] (usually their family farm and hence their 'back garden'). No wonder schools are less likely to arrange farm visits and farmers are increasingly anxious about the public. Even so, farming is part of our heritage and it is vital to have a real understanding about where much of our food comes from. Here are a few ways to reconnect your children with farming:

- Take part in initiatives such as Open Farm Sunday held every June.

- Visit agricultural and country shows and don't just go on the helter-skelter – get close to livestock.

- Immerse yourself in rural life for a family holiday where the kids will hunt for eggs for your breakfast and milk a cow before lunch. Look out for child-friendly farm stays.

- Enjoy Tractor Ted books and DVDs – they show modern farming images and contain lots of fascinating facts. Because they are designed for farmers' children, there is no gloss and they even feature humungous piles of steaming manure.

- For older children, try *From Farm to Table* by Richard and Louise Spilsbury. This colourful and informative book looks at the real stories behind food production, with lots of pointers for family discussions.

- For an older readers' chapter book, *Farm Boy* by Michael Morpurgo is a wonderful tale spanning three generations that really evokes rural life and the relationship between a farmer and the land.

An ode to the egg

Eggs have provided me with many a quick scrambled dinner for hungry tummies and are packed full of B vitamins, which help us to gain our energy from food, support the immune system and enable the formation of red-blood cells. They are also a great source of vitamins A and D. Previous advice on limiting your egg intake has been overruled, because it is now known that the cholesterol they contain does not significantly impact blood cholesterol levels.

If you are pregnant, well-cooked eggs are fine. They contain folate, which is essential for your growing babe. Do buy free-range eggs though, or you are supporting battery farming.

It was only when my children had the chance to visit a friend's hens that I really learnt to appreciate the egg. The children reached their hands cautiously into nests to find the still-warm orbs, which they carefully placed in a basket, eyes large with wonder.

'But where do the eggs come out, Mummy?'
'Does it hurt the hen?'

Then we watched the chicks hatching out under the incubator light.

Next, we baked a cake.

'Are there chicks in our eggs, Mummy?'
'Why not?'

We broke vivid golden yolks in the bowl, and blended them simply with butter, flour, baking powder and sugar. We watched our cake rising in the oven, golden and miraculous, and ate while it was still warm, watching the chickens peck around outside.

'Do we eat chickens like those ones?'
'But do they have to get dead first?'

The egg is a perfectly packaged lesson in reproduction, a direct link to our food, and a cheap, healthy ingredient. If you have space to keep hens, you'll have an endless source of nutrition and entertainment. I'll leave it to you to tackle all those tricky questions!

Perfectly packaged

Footnotes for Chapter 3

1 Lifestyles statistics team (2014). 'Statistics on obesity, physical activity and diet'. Health and Social Care Information Centre. http://www.hscic.gov.uk/catalogue/PUB13648/Obes-phys-acti-diet-eng-2014-rep.pdf

2 Baby-Led Weaning. (2015). 'Welcome to baby-led weaning'. http://www.babyledweaning.com

3 Caton, S. J. et al. (2014). 'Learning to eat vegetables in early life: the role of timing, age and individual eating traits'. University of Leeds, Plos One.
http://www.plosone.org/article/info%3Adoi%2F10.1371%2Fjournal.pone.0097609

4 Thomas, P. et al. (2010). 'Healthy planet eating, how lower meat diets can save lives and the planet'. Friends of the Earth. http://www.foe.co.uk/sites/default/files/downloads/healthy_planet_eating.pdf.
Based on research by Oxford University.

5 UN Food and Agriculture Organization (2006). 'Livestock a major threat to environment'.
http://www.fao.org/newsroom/en/news/2006/1000448/index.html

6 Institution of Mechanical Engineers (2013). 'Global food: waste not, want not'.
http://www.imeche.org/knowledge/themes/environment/global-food

7 Love Food Hate Waste (2014). 'The facts about food waste'.
http://england.lovefoodhatewaste.com/node/2472

8 NFU (2011). 'Safety focus on: children on farms'. http://www.nfuonline.com/assets/7222

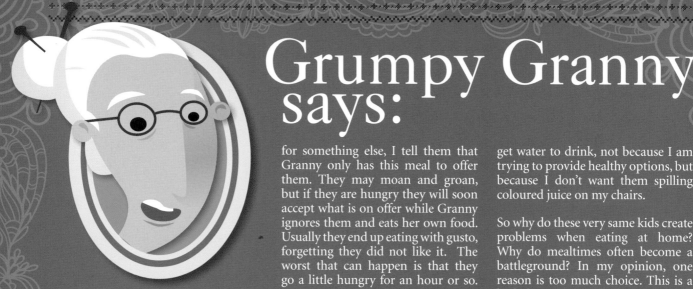

Grumpy Granny says:

Choose less choice

It's simple – if you are hungry you will want to eat. Yet parents will often try to shove another spoonful of food into a baby who does not want it. Why?

A child who does not want food is either ill, or they have learnt from their over-attentive parents that food can be used as a brilliant weapon to ensure undivided adult attention. Alternatively, they are not hungry. When they refuse food or they refuse to try something new, it usually means they are full up from previous eating opportunities.

When my grandchildren visit me, sometimes they complain that they do not like what is on offer. I take no notice and tell them to eat what they want and to leave the rest. I do not offer substitutes and if they ask for something else, I tell them that Granny only has this meal to offer them. They may moan and groan, but if they are hungry they will soon accept what is on offer while Granny ignores them and eats her own food. Usually they end up eating with gusto, forgetting they did not like it. The worst that can happen is that they go a little hungry for an hour or so.

Mealtimes with the grandchildren are usually a pleasure. I provide good unprocessed food for lunch or dinner but will spoil them at afternoon tea with homemade cake or biscuits, preferably ones they have helped to make themselves. They only ever

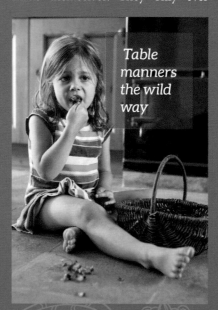

Table manners the wild way

get water to drink, not because I am trying to provide healthy options, but because I don't want them spilling coloured juice on my chairs.

So why do these very same kids create problems when eating at home? Why do mealtimes often become a battleground? In my opinion, one reason is too much choice. This is a bad idea, whether they are two or ten years old. It might be OK to ask the older child if they would like pasta or fish, a manageable choice, but open-ended questions are a disaster: 'What would you like for lunch?' Or, in a restaurant, 'What would you like to eat?' It does not work. Multiple options create stress.

Kids do not like to think they are losing out, so giving them choice causes them tension. If they choose one thing, they are rejecting something else which may be better. This is hard to accept, especially when you do not have enough knowledge to make the best decision. No wonder they end up having a tantrum.

Being a parent means managing the world your child experiences. Less choice brings gains for everyone: it means less wasted food, which is good for the environment; it means an easier life for parents; and it establishes good eating habits which will benefit children for the rest of their lives.

Hunter-gatherer

4

Foraging is a good excuse for time outdoors together

Let me tell you about a little shop I know. It's just down the road and is stocked with the very best seasonal produce that is as fresh as can be. Oh, and all the food is free – you simply help yourself. The proprietor is very well respected in environmental circles, and goes by the name of Mother Nature.

If that sounds a bit too good to be true, I'm not talking about some fancy organic store for celebrities that you can't access, but something we can all do. Simply get out and about in the countryside, looking for edible plants, fruits and nuts. Free stuff is always satisfying, but foraging for dinner is also a wonderful way of exploring your local area, learning about nature and discovering your inner hunter-gatherer.

Wild food is the greenest imaginable – it is seasonal and free from pesticides, herbicides, packaging and food miles. Unlike growing your own, the hard labour has already been done by nature. It is worth remembering that once upon a time, all food was wild and uncultivated.

At first you may wander aimlessly, wondering if you can make grass soup, but soon you'll be spotting edible opportunities and experimenting with more unusual ingredients. It really makes you look at your world differently. In early May I will spot elderflower everywhere, and watch the buds for that perfect moment when they burst into creamy fragrant flowers.

Many foods you can forage have incredible levels of nutrition that out-perform supermarket-bought 'super-foods' such as broccoli and spinach. Nettles, for example, are packed with calcium, potassium and vitamin C. Given that it is often a matter of minutes from picking to plate, you also know that all the goodness is maximized.

Children delight in foraging. The desire to pick something up and taste it is innate – we spend a lot of effort training infants out of this practice, so foraging can feel like a leap of faith. Your carefully constructed boundaries can become complicated as you try to explain 'those berries will make you poorly but these ones are good for you'. In my experience, children over the age of three can understand this and soon learn what is OK to eat. Your absolute rule can be to check with an adult before tasting anything. Those younger than three need close supervision with this activity, as they do with pretty much anything.

Children behave very differently with food that they have found and collected themselves. Blackberries out of a supermarket tub would be considered too tangy by my children, but when picked straight off the bush (even the ones that, to my eyes, look a little under-ripe) are declared amazing.

It's a good basis for imaginative play too. Pretend you are lost in the woods and to survive you will need to find your own food. For older children, it's a chance to be an intrepid adventurer like Bear Grylls or Ray Mears.

Foraging is one of those educational activities where the purpose makes the learning fun. You can take a guide book, looking for details that help you identify a specimen and work through identification keys together. Foraging is also a great chance to talk about risk and how you decide if something is safe to do.

Let's face it, foraging is never going to replace the weekly shop, and many a time you will come back from your foray empty-handed. Nevertheless, what you and your family will have gained is exercise, a sense of adventure and a deeper understanding of your environment.

Now that is worth muddy boots and a few bramble scratches!

Foraging guidelines and **safety**

Only eat plants and fruits you are 100% sure that you have correctly identified. There are only two mushrooms I will eat (giant puffball and penny bun) because the others are too complicated for my current level of knowledge. The risk of getting it wrong is not worth it, especially where children are concerned.

I would also avoid most wild food when pregnant – for example, pine needles can induce miscarriage in some animals but would be fine normally (pine needle tea is lovely). Always carry a good field guide with detailed illustrations. Double-check online at home with the plant in your hands.

Avoid roadsides and paths: traffic fumes and dog wee don't make great accompaniments to dinner. Dog faeces contains the eggs of the dangerous *Toxocara canis* worm so avoid areas where there could be dog muck. Wash your produce carefully too, to remove grit, dirt and little creatures.

The golden rule for foraging is never to take the whole plant or all the berries or nuts. Leave some for wildlife and to ensure it is still alive and thriving the next time you want a little wildness for dinner.

Children and adults should wear trousers, wellies and long sleeves for foraging, as you will often find yourselves wading through long grass or reaching through prickles. Gloves are vital for sweet chestnut and nettle collection.

So off you merrily go into the countryside, helping yourself to nature's bounty ... but hang on, is it nature's bounty or Mr Smith's – are you in fact stealing? Are you allowed to forage without being a criminal? The Theft Act of 1968 created a number of offences against property in England and Wales and states that:

'A person who picks mushrooms growing wild on any land, or who picks flowers, fruit or foliage from a plant growing wild on any land, does not (although not in possession of the land) steal what he picks, unless he does it for reward or for sale or other commercial purpose.'

The Scottish Outdoor Access Code has a similar ethos. In short, intended use is what counts, so no selling your amazing nettle muffins please. Do make sure you have permission to be on the land, and don't stray too far from public rights of ways such as footpaths unless you have first checked with the landowner.

If you are intending to forage abroad, investigate the country's laws first.

Urban **jungle**

Maybe you live in a city and think this is not exactly relevant for you ... well, think again! The average city park could contain over 50 edible species. To get started, look out for sweet chestnut or hazelnut trees and brambles for blackberries. Dandelions and stinging nettles are readily available, from car parks to under hedges.

Foraging in cities comes with an extra note of caution about pollution. Avoid areas right next to busy roads, wash food carefully and consume in moderation.

Mushrooms are like sponges and can soak up fumes and toxins, so target their country cousins instead. Avoid areas that may have been sprayed with herbicides, pick above dog-wee height and don't forget that even in a city park many plants may be poisonous, so be sure to identify plants carefully.

Forager in
training

Part of the beauty of foraging is learning to see your environment in a different way. After all, if something is going to go into your mouth, you want to have a good look at it first.

For children, you can encourage the skill of careful looking in their everyday play outside. It's the treasure-hunt principle and has saved many a dull walk. Simply set them a challenge to find items such as a pine cone, an acorn, a green leaf, a yellow leaf and a pebble. This can be done on the walk to school (leave earlier than usual) or in the smallest of urban parks.

If you want to be a bit more prepared about it, feely cards are a lovely activity.

'To be honest, Mum, I prefer my cheese straws'

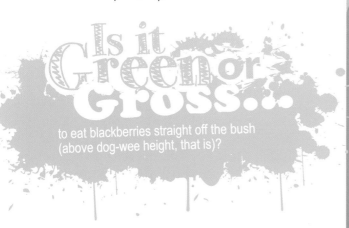

Is it Green or Gross...

to eat blackberries straight off the bush (above dog-wee height, that is)?

Green [CHALLENGE] #10

Can you find something edible in your garden? (The vegetable patch doesn't count.) This challenge could be called 'eat your weeds'. Try dandelion leaves, ground elder, clover, nasturtium leaves or fat hen. If all else fails, you can chew on the delicate end of a fresh blade of grass.

Dandelion petals are good in pancakes

Feely cards

Cover a square of card in double-sided tape and on one side stick man-made textures, such as corrugated cardboard, sandpaper and silky fabric. Challenge the child to find matching textures in nature to stick on the other side. You can also try this with colours.

Your foraging year – for beginners and **accompanied children**

Here is a rough guide to plants you can collect throughout the year. Remember, their availability will depend on the weather and location.

Make sure you look up each item in a field guide before you start.

January: dandelions

If your garden is anything like mine, you won't have to go far to find dandelions! You can also find them in many parks most of the year round.

Dandelions are great for learner-foragers because they are easy to find. Growing in rosettes of jagged leaves, the bright-yellow flowers stand out like beacons. The whole plant is edible, but the leaves are good to start with. They can be bitter when mature, so look for the tender young leaves that appear very early in springtime. Dandelions contain more beta-carotene than carrots and more iron and calcium than spinach.

Foraging for dandelion leaves

In French, the dandelion is often known as *pissenlit* ('piss in the bed'). Are those taunting playground cries of 'you touched a dandelion so you're going to wet the bed' correct? There is a grain of truth behind this folklore because the dandelion is mildly diuretic, but a child would need to drink large quantities of dandelion tea to experience this soggy side-effect.

Dandelion leaves are yummy in a goat's cheese salad and also go very well with crispy bacon. My children find salad leaves generally repulsive but they are prepared to try the petals because they think it is funny to eat a flower. If you have similar issues, try these ideas:

Dandelion pancakes

First, make the basic pancake batter below and then decide if you want sweet or savoury pancakes.

Makes 14-16 large pancakes

1 tbsp butter, melted, and extra for frying

2 free-range eggs

300ml milk

100g plain flour (or wholemeal for a change)

Simply mix the ingredients together until smooth. Rest the batter for half an hour (while you pick those dandelions).

Now decide if you are going sweet (you need flower heads) or savoury (you'll need the leaves).

Sweet pancakes

For the sweet version, mix the petals of a few dandelions in to the pancake batter just before cooking. Cook as usual (frying in a little butter) and serve with honey or maple syrup.

Savoury pancakes

Simply add a handful of finely chopped dandelion leaves to the pancake batter just before cooking then season with a little salt and pepper, and cook as usual. Serve with a rich Cheddar cheese sauce.

February: sea beet

February is not the best month for foraging, so if you're new to the game, you may wish to hang on until springtime … but if you are a hardy family, head to a coastline for this green treat.

Sea beet grows exclusively in coastal areas and all parts of it are edible, including the summertime flowers and even the roots. It makes a great replacement for any recipe where you can use spinach or chard. At the coast, along footpaths, on cliff tops, in sand and by pebbles, look out for a plant with bright green shiny leaves, up to one metre high.

Try this yummy frittata for dinner:

Sea beet and ricotta frittata

Serves 4

400g potatoes, peeled and sliced 1cm thick

6 free-range eggs

Salt and pepper

100g ricotta

150g sea beet leaves, cleaned and shredded

1 tbsp rapeseed oil

1 red pepper, thinly sliced

50g grated Cheddar

Boil the potatoes for 10 minutes or so until tender. Beat the eggs in a large bowl and season with salt and pepper. Add the ricotta cheese and mix until partially combined (lumps are expected). Steam the sea beet (over the potato pan is fine) until wilted. Squeeze out any excess moisture from the sea beet and drain the potatoes.

Now heat the rapeseed oil in a large non-stick frying pan, add the pepper slices and fry for 2 minutes. Next, add in the potatoes and cook for a further 2 minutes.

Mix the sea beet into the egg mix and pour into the frying pan, quickly stirring to combine all the ingredients. Allow it to cook for five minutes on a low heat while preheating the grill.

Pop the grated Cheddar on top, then grill for 3 minutes or so, until the cheese has melted and the egg mixture is firm. Serve hot or cold.

March: wild garlic
(also known as ramsons)

Wild garlic is great for children because the flavour is milder than normal garlic. Unlike domestic garlic where the bulb is eaten, it is the leaves of the wild garlic that are best to use.

Head to deciduous woodland, the older the better, and use your nose and eyes. Look out for white starry flowers with pointed petals (in springtime) and a strong scent of garlic, particularly if you walk over the leaves. This plant grows up to 45cm tall and carpets woodland floors. The leaves are best picked when young – March is the perfect month.

Do not to confuse wild garlic with the poisonous lily of the valley – they look similar but the leaves of the lily don't smell garlicky so it's easy to tell the difference.

Wild garlic works well when added to a tomato sauce for pasta or pizza, and the flowers are stunning when added to salads.

This simple recipe gives garlic bread a more subtle flavour, and an elegance that elevates it from a 1980s staple to a modern dinner-party talking point.

Wild garlic bread
. . . .
Serves 4–6

Brush extra virgin olive oil across a sliced loaf of bread such as focaccia or sourdough. Pop under the grill until lightly toasted on both sides. Sprinkle with a handful of finely chopped wild garlic leaves, another glug of olive oil, a little sea salt and pepper and some grated Cheddar cheese if you fancy it. Then return to the grill for a minute (or until cheese is bubbling).

Wild garlic leaves can also be finely chopped then mixed with butter and baked in a baguette wrapped in foil.

Stinging nettles – do you dare?

April: stinging nettles

I love stinging nettles! They are one of the most vital native plants for wildlife, providing shelter and food for over 40 species of insects including beautiful butterflies such as the peacock. It is the sting that makes it such a safe place for insect life because not much is going to disturb them. Nettles taste delicious too.

Nettles are almost everywhere and can be found on most 'edges': of fields, on verges, along streams, woodland fringes, throughout wasteland, and maybe even at the bottom of your garden. The tenacious nettle requires little to survive, and where it does, it brings wildlife. Up close it has surprisingly pretty heart-shaped leaves with a serrated edge, covered in fine, stinging hairs.

Foraging for nettles is a bit like bungee jumping versus having afternoon tea (or picking elderflower). The key is having the right kit and it is vital that you wear gloves, longsleeves and trousers. Nettle hunting is not a glamorous occupation and some swear by washing-up gloves. This probably isn't one for children under five to help with, as there is a decent likelihood of a sting or two creeping through your layers and some resilience is required.

Take scissors or secateurs and just pick the top six or so leaves, as they can get a bit tough lower down. It is best to pick nettles before they have flowered and become bitter, so avoid after June.

Nettle soup is the traditional recipe for these beauties – highly nutritious and vivid green, it is reminiscent of spinach soup (just cook the nettles with potatoes, onions, stock and serve with a spoon of Greek yoghurt). I award 10 out of 10 to you as an incredible parent if you can persuade your kids to eat it. Mine wouldn't touch the stuff, even if I said it was alien slime, so I invented a little recipe which they can't get enough of: nettle muffins.

Alternatively, nettles can replace spinach in any recipe (where cooking is required. Raw nettles would be … interesting).

Preparing nettles

Wearing washing-up gloves, give your nettles a good rinse in cold water and put in a large pan. Cook until wilted and then, when cooled a little, squeeze out the excess water either using a sieve or kitchen roll. They are now stingless! Next, cut them up fairly finely. Once cooked, nettles freeze well.

Nettle muffins

Makes 12 muffins

A carrier bag full of nettles, prepared as above (you'll need about 100g once prepared so you may have some nettles left over to freeze)

2 free-range eggs

240ml milk

50g melted butter

100g mature Cheddar, grated

250g plain flour

2 tsp baking powder

½ tsp salt

Preheat the oven to 180°C or gas mark 4 and grease a muffin or cupcake tin (or fill with cases).

Whisk together the eggs, milk, melted butter and cheese. Separately, combine the flour, baking powder and salt and stir this into the wet mixture until well mixed (don't worry if it looks lumpy). Now add the chopped nettles and stir through.

Simply spoon into the tin, making sure you don't overfill each cup – about two-thirds full is perfect.

Now bake until the muffins are golden-brown. Cool on a wire rack or gobble up straightaway.

May: clover

Red and white clover may be hated by 'stripy lawn' gardeners but they are great plants for bees. They are very pretty too, with their patterned leaves and bobble-like flowers. You can find them on lawns and most grassland, and they are especially easy to spot when flowering from late May until July.

Both red and white clover is edible, flowers and leaves alike, and packed full of nutrients. I've found many four-leaved clovers while foraging for clover, so you may just get lucky.

Red clover lemonade

This is a lovely refreshing drink.

Serves 4

3 cups red clover blossoms

4 cups water

1 cup lemon juice

6-8 tbsp of honey to taste

Add the blossoms to the water in a pan and simmer for five minutes. Let it cool a little, then strain. Stir in the lemon juice and honey until well mixed. Chill before serving.

Red clover makes beautiful dusky pink lemonade

Children will enjoy collecting the fragrant blossom of the elder tree

June: elderflowers

Elderflowers are the blossom of the elder tree, which flowers from mid-May until the beginning of July. The saucer-sized flower heads, a fragrant mass of petals, are distinctive and easy to collect.

This is the perfect foraging task for children. Beady little eyes are great at identifying the flowers at the right stage – just burst into bloom is perfect, with no discoloured petals. The flower heads are tender enough to be snapped off by hand if you don't want to use tools (although being trusted with grown-up tools can bring out the best in many children). Younger ones can shake the blossoms to get any insects out.

Elderflower cordial

This is deliciously refreshing and popular with children. It's also a lovely ingredient: you'll find yourself adding a glug or two to the rhubarb for a crumble, stirring it through Greek yoghurt or popping a little on a summer fruit salad.

Makes approximately 3 litres of cordial

20 elderflower heads

2.5kg caster sugar

1.5 litres water

2 unwaxed lemons (or try 3 limes for a refreshing alternative)

80g citric acid (available from pharmacies or online)

A clean fine cloth (such as muslin or a tea towel) and a large sieve

Give the elderflowers a good shake and rinse to remove any dirt or creepy-crawlies. Pop them in a large bowl, with the main stalks trimmed off. Boil the sugar and water in a pan, stirring until the sugar has completely dissolved. Meanwhile, zest the lemons, then cut the lemons into chunks and add both to the elderflowers.

Allow the sugar syrup to cool a little before pouring into the bowl over the flowers and lemons, and then stir in the citric acid. Cover with a cloth or cling film and leave at room temperature for 48 hours, stirring occasionally.

After a couple of days, remove the large bits of flower and fruit, and strain the cordial through a sieve lined with fine muslin or a clean tea towel (or a pair of clean tights!). Pour into sterilized glass bottles (wash in soapy water or the dishwasher, then dry in a low oven to sterilize).

Store in the fridge or a cool pantry. The cordial will keep for three months while sealed, but once you open a bottle, store in the fridge and consume within a month. Alternatively, freeze in an ice-cube tray or bag to have portion-ready amounts all year round.

Serve diluted with iced water or fizzy water (also rather good with sparkling wine).

Elderflower cordial –
summer in a glass

July: seaweed and marsh samphire

Seaweed is packed full of vitamins and minerals, and can be collected from any coastline with exposed rocks. It is delicious added to risottos, soups and bread, or simply sliced thinly and fried until crispy.

When gathering seaweed, make sure you leave the roots on the rocks so it can regrow. If you have any seaweed left over after dinner, it can be hilarious to add some to the bath for some slippery slimy entertainment.

Look out for sea lettuce, which is common and looks like shiny crumpled lettuce or cabbage leaves.

Marsh samphire is my favourite food in the whole world. It isn't technically seaweed but a tasty succulent, also known as sea asparagus. In recent years it has become a trendy vegetable, commanding high prices for a mere sprig on a plate.

It is easy to find on marshland at the coast and despite being green and nutritious, I find that children love it. It may be because it is impossible to eat in an elegant fashion – you slurp the cooked samphire off the plant, leaving a tough strand behind, and getting butter down your chin.

As with seaweed, just pinch or snip off the tops of the plants, leaving the gritty fibrous stems in the ground to regrow. Try a little straight from the marsh too – salty and succulent.

Rock samphire is also edible, and tasty, but it is less common and often grows on rocks, at height, so collecting it can be too risky.

Simply delicious samphire

Serves 4

Half a carrier bag of samphire (this is a feast for four)

Unsalted butter

A splash of malt vinegar or a squeeze of lemon

Carefully remove the root or anything that's not bright green, such as the plant's stems. Make sure you give it a really good rinse to get rid of grit, sand and excess salt.

It's best to boil the samphire in plenty of fresh water (no need to add salt). I've tried steaming it but the end result is too salty. Cook for approximately four minutes until tender and it slides off the inner stem.

It is wonderful served simply: piled in a bowl with knobs of unsalted butter and a little lemon juice or malt vinegar (although my children prefer just butter).

Seaside-foraging safety

You'll find more seaweed when the tide is low but do be aware of the tides (check online) and ensure that there is no risk of being cut off from land.

If you are hunting for samphire on salt marshes or mudflats, do not roam too far from a path. The mud can be very sticky – welly boot loss is practically inevitable and some areas can be deep.

to eat hawthorn leaves? See if your children like them (they are very good for you but even the young leaves have a strong flavour).

How will you eat yours?

>> **Top 10 ways** to ...
use blackberries

1. In a crumble. Wonderful with peach or plum too (try adding 75g of ground almonds to the topping for extra protein and flavour).

2. In muffins, with a little lemon zest and some poppy seeds.

3. Just for grown-ups ... crush a few and add the juice to a glass of bubbly for a Brambleini.

4. Cooked with duck or venison.

5. Mixed with honey and Greek yogurt.

6. As a compote, served with pancakes.

7. On your morning porridge.

8. With thick double cream as a filling in a Victoria sponge.

9. As a bramble pavlova, replacing summer berries such as strawberries. Fresh blackberries instead of syrupy cherries also update the black forest gateau.

10. As a spiced blackberry chutney – lovely with cheese or cold meats.

Safe to eat – a correctly identified puffball mushroom

August: giant puffballs

August is a lovely month for foraging. It's fruit and nut time, with blackberries and hazelnuts ripening in the hedgerows. Hazelnuts are ripe when the leaf surrounding them is starting to turn yellowish, but move fast, as it will always be a case of you versus the squirrels in the race to the nut.

The puffball is a white globe that can grow as big as your head. This sounds like something from a Roald Dahl book, and probably a revolting vegetable that the BFG had to eat. In fact, the puffball has a tasty, earthy flavour and an unusual texture that when cooked is like a mix between a savoury marshmallow and firm tofu. Due to its size, it can actually be used as a football if you don't fancy eating it (or if it is a bit old to eat – the young ones are best).

This magnificent and entertaining fungus is also the safest way to introduce some wild mushroom into your diet because it is so easy to identify. Do make sure it is still pure white throughout. As they age, they become yellow and taste bitter.

The puffball is very versatile and can be used like any mushroom; stir-fried, cooked in garlic butter, in soups, baked or grilled. My favourite way is as a very healthy pizza base, making this a low-carb, wheat-free way to enjoy pizza.

Puffball pizza

Customize with your own favourite toppings, but here is a basic puffball margherita.

Serves 4

A giant puffball the size of your head (smaller is fine too)!

I medium-sized onion, finely chopped

Salt and pepper

2 cloves garlic, finely chopped

400g tin chopped tomatoes

2 tbsp tomato puree

1 tsp dried oregano

Pinch of sugar

1 ball of mozzarella, shredded

1 tbsp olive oil for the sauce. More will be needed for brushing the puffball slices.

Heat a saucepan over a medium heat and add the oil. Once hot, add the onion and a pinch of salt and fry for four to five minutes until softened. Add the garlic and cook for a further two minutes.

Pour in the tomatoes and tomato purée and season with salt and pepper, the oregano and a pinch of sugar. Reduce the heat and simmer gently for 20-30 minutes until the sauce has thickened to a jam-like consistency.

Next, slice your puffball into rounds about 2cm thick … each of these discs is a pizza base.

Heat the grill to hot. Brush oil onto both sides of the puffball slices, season with salt and pepper and grill for two to three minutes each side until soft.

Now top with the tomato sauce and mozzarella (and any other toppings you fancy). Grill until the cheese is melted and bubbling, which should take 2-3 minutes.

Puffball safety

The giant puffball is the easiest mushroom to identify but double-check that:

- cut from bottom to top, it is pure white throughout;
- it is bigger than a grapefruit;
- you have looked at pictures of common earthball mushrooms and young fly agaric (when they first grow, they form an egg-sized 'puff') and ruled them out. These poisonous fungi look similar to the puffball when young, but if your puffball meets the top two criteria, then you can be confident it is a genuine puffball.

Check your mushrooms online: www.wildfooduk.com has useful images and descriptions to help you.

September: elderberry

Dark red-black clusters of elderberry fruit will be ripe by September and can be found in most woodland or in hedgerows. Packed full of potassium, calcium and vitamin C, they are highly nutritious. They are most commonly used for more adult recipes, such as chutney or wine, and are often overlooked as a pudding ingredient.

The only rules with elderberries are: however temping they look, don't eat them raw – they can make some people nauseous; and make sure they are dark in colour, as the unripe green berries aren't good for tummies.

On an alcoholic note, I can't help but mention the dark sloes gracing our hedgerows at this time of year. The fabulous sloe gin really is Ribena for grown-ups and is so warming and fortifying. (A sneaky recipe for sloe gin … Pick enough sloes to half fill a bottle, freeze them, pop them into the sterilized bottle with a couple of large tablespoons of caster sugar, fill to the top with decent gin and leave for 10 weeks, shaking or turning the bottle every couple of days.)

Elderberry and apple crumble

Serves 4

2 clusters of elderberries, washed

500g cooking apples

100g caster sugar

50g oats

150g flour

100g butter

1 tsp ground cinnamon

100g soft brown sugar

Preheat the oven to 180°C or gas mark 4.

Peel, core and slice the apples and arrange in an ovenproof dish. Pull the berries from their stalks and add these to the apples. Sprinkle over the caster sugar and give a little stir.

Rub the butter into the flour, oats, cinnamon and brown sugar until crumbly, then pour this on top of the fruit and gently pat down.

Bake for 35-40 minutes until the fruit is tender and the top is golden-brown.

October: sweet chestnuts

Collecting sweet chestnuts in an autumnal wood really brings out my inner hunter-gatherer. That feeling of being on the cusp of winter creates an animal urge to find delicious and nutritious food. (Hibernating would be nice too, but you can't have it all!)

Sweet chestnuts are not to be confused with horse chestnuts (inedible conkers). Their nuts look quite different: the conkers are surrounded by soft, stubby spikes, while the sweet chestnut has a casing of longer, more hair-like spikes and you will need gloves to handle them.

You'll find sweet chestnuts in deciduous woodland and in parks. My local swimming pool has lots in the car park and my children have worked out that swimming hats make reasonable hand protectors for collecting them.

The nuts can be stored in a cool place until Christmas if they are perfect (with no holes or cracks). If you'd rather not chance it, freeze them. To prepare the nuts for freezing, boil them for five minutes, then drain and place in cold water. Peel them pronto, as the skins will come off easiest now. Little dextrous fingers are helpful here, but you will need to start each one off with a sharp knife. Then just pop the peeled chestnuts into the freezer until you are ready to use them.

Sweet chestnuts

My nan's Christmas stuffing

As a vegetarian for many of my teenage years, this stuffing replaced turkey at my Christmas meal. Everyone else dug in too, of course, and it is excellent in turkey sandwiches or for enriching turkey soup on Boxing Day.

I always helped my grandmother to peel the chestnuts. She also made the brandy butter, and Christmas without these two homemade accompaniments is unimaginable.

This stuffing is for chestnut purists and it is the easiest recipe around. It isn't the ideal stuffing to use in your turkey but is lovely baked separately or used in goose.

You will need:

Approximately 6 mugs of fresh chestnuts with the skins on (or 4 mugs of the pre-frozen ones)

2 tbsp salted butter, melted

pepper

a splash of milk

Preheat the oven to 180°C or gas mark 4.

Boil and peel the chestnuts as detailed above. Crush the chestnuts roughly with a fork (you want to keep some texture) then add the butter, a grind or two of pepper and a splash of milk. This should form a sticky (but not runny) mash. Put this into a greased baking dish (or keep refrigerated for stuffing a goose) and pat down and pattern with a fork.

This can then be baked for 15-20 minutes with the rest of your Christmas dinner.

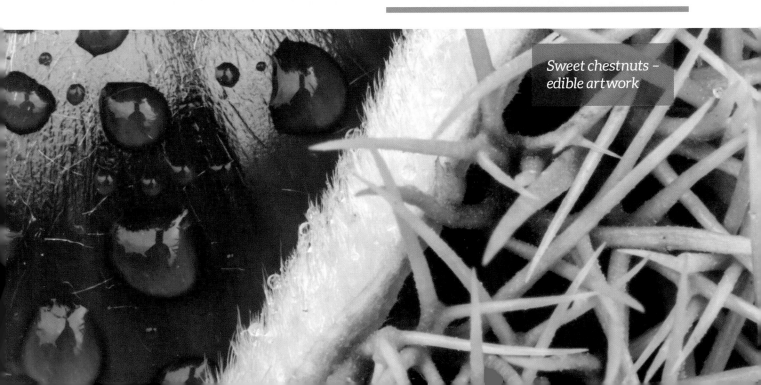

Sweet chestnuts – edible artwork

Rosehips make a delicious syrup

November–December: rosehips

Do forgive me for lumping these two months together. There is still a lot of wild food that you can forage out there, but it becomes decreasingly child-friendly and less suitable for beginner foragers over the next few months.

At this time of year the lovely rosehip is easy to spot and collect. Shining bright-red from the hedgerows, they are jewels among the frost, and are packed full of vitamin C (20 times more so than oranges) to help you beat all those winter germs. During the Second World War they were used as a replacement for citrus fruits.

Look for them in hedgerows, but do watch out for thorns. They should be collected after the first frost.

Rosehip syrup

Exotic, sweet and fruity, this syrup tastes more like it comes from the Caribbean than your icy hedgerow. Children will enjoy it, and a spoonful for poorly little ones will cheer them up if nothing else. Diluted with water, it is a lovely cordial and has lots of grown-up cocktail potential too (fab with vodka).

I love to use it instead of honey on pancakes, waffles, rice pudding or stirred into that warming bowl of morning porridge for a vitamin C hit.

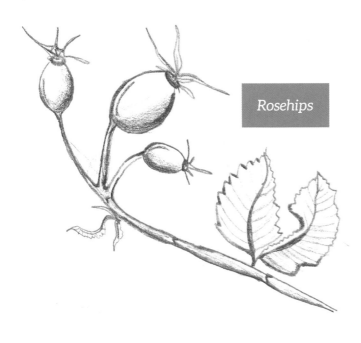

Rosehips

Save the strained juice to the side, and put the rosehip pulp back in the saucepan, with more water. You will need half the volume of water that you used to start the recipe. Repeat the original process: bring to the boil, remove from heat and allow to infuse again for 20 minutes. Strain as before.

Now mix the two sets of strained juice and bring to the boil in a clean pan. You'll need to simmer until the quantity has halved, then remove it from the heat. Stir in the sugar until dissolved before bringing back to the boil a final time, for a five-minute simmer. Done!

Store in sterilized and sealed jars or small bottles and keep refrigerated once opened.

You will need:

As many rosehips as you can find

Water (to double the rosehip weight – so if you have 500g rosehips you need 1 litre of water). You'll need a bit more water later too

A clean fine cloth (such as muslin or a tea towel) and a large sieve

Caster sugar (to match the weight of the rosehips)

Wash and chop the rosehips and bring the water to the boil in a large pan. Add in the rosehips, return to the boil, then take off the heat and cover with a lid. This needs to infuse for half an hour – stir occasionally.

After it has infused, strain through a sieve lined with the cloth, over a large bowl. This should take about an hour, and a little stir every now and again can help.

If you are keen to find out more about wild foods, Richard Mabey's book *Food for Free* (available as a pocket-sized Collins gem edition) is a brilliant companion.

Green [CHALLENGE] #11

Foraging can be about finding useful items as well as yummy food. See if you can find natural chalk stones. If you have a gravel drive, you are on to a winner. Otherwise, try a beach with chalk cliffs. Chalk is great for patio art and decorating fences and trees because it will just wash away. Did you know that chalk is white because it is formed from the colourless skeletons of marine plankton?

Grumpy Granny says:

Why turn down a free meal?

Families are short of money; fruit and veg are good for you; locally sourced food is ethically sound: so why aren't more people out foraging for free food while teaching their children about nature and getting exercise as well?

It's because they think food has to be processed or pre-packed or, at the very least, displayed in a wicker basket resting on a bed of straw at the local deli or farm shop. This generation has forgotten that plants grow wild naturally and some can be eaten and will taste really good. The problem is they carry no sell-by date, no analysis of calories and nutritional content, no name of someone to sue if they contain a slug, snail or other interesting item of wildlife.

Wild food is there for the picking

A perfect example is the blackberry. They are found throughout the country and a half-hour pick can easily result in a kilo of fruit. They will be smaller than the supermarket fruit but the flavour will be more intense and the price difference considerable: free compared with over £12 for a kilo in a shop.

Saving money is only part of it. Your children will learn to be careful or the prickles of the blackberry will hurt them. They will inevitably wipe their fingers on their T-shirts and discover that blackberry juice makes a fantastic and indelible stain. They will realize the link between plants and food and themselves, and why nature matters. They will be out in the countryside getting exercise, and parents will be entertaining them without spending money.

Instead, I see yummy mummies with manicured nails buying imported organic blackberries from Spain at the supermarket. Even those who are struggling financially still ignore the free food around them. People seem to think food has to have been collected and distributed by someone else before it can be eaten. Food does not need to be sold through a retailer to be good. Just try hazelnuts or sweet chestnuts picked from the tree.

Teaching a child how to find, pick, cook and eat their food is so important. Foraging is about much much more than free food.

Body talk

Let's talk about healthy bodies and minds

5

A natural, active pregnancy involves lots of time outdoors

And now I have to make an upfront confession. You see, somewhere out there is a landfill site filled with my son's nappies. They are disposables destined to sit there for more than 500 years, failing to rot and polluting our environment.

I didn't use reusable nappies.

Further on in my parenting journey, I have met many people who love reusable nappies and have given me many tips. I wish I'd known them at the time. So what went wrong for me?

Being thrifty by nature, I acquired an assorted muddle of nappies from various secondhand sources. Few of them fitted my son properly and I was put off by the leaks and also the (early) toddler diarrhoea. The couple that didn't leak I used, but of course they were often in the wash. As the tiredness kicked in, and then I returned to work, it just seemed easier to let the disposables take over.

So that's my confession over with, phew! This chapter will help you succeed where I have failed. Luckily for my conscience, there is far more to looking after your child's health and body in an eco-friendly way than how you deal with wee and poo. So read on and find out how to look after your child as naturally as possible.

A natural
pregnancy

When you are pregnant, you suddenly stop and look at your life. You know it is about to change beyond recognition and also you are so aware of the baby you are already responsible for. It is the start of a lifetime of rules, regulations and advice that will come your way. Don't eat this, don't sleep in that position, don't wear underwired bras… There are so many guidelines and it can be hard to decide which to care about. The important ones your doctor or midwife will tell you, so you probably already know that you need to take folic acid supplements and that alcohol, cigarettes, drugs, too much caffeine or certain foods could harm your unborn baby.

But what next? Where are you going to draw the line to protect your unborn child? Will you eat only organic food? Wear organic breathable fibres? Or maybe you should stop wearing cosmetics and dyeing your hair? If you want to get it right, it may feel that life is one long list of bad things waiting to happen if you make a tiny lapse in judgement.

All this can make you feel stressed, and then you feel even more worried because you know that the cortisol and adrenalin that you produce when you are anxious are not ideal for the chilled baby you want to make.

What does a natural baby need?

>> Top 5 tips for … a natural green pregnancy

1. Spend time in nature and try listening to birdsong.
2. Stay active unless otherwise advised by your doctor but also make time to rest and relax regularly.
3. If you are worried about chemicals, search online for brands of nail polish and hair dye marketed at pregnant women.
4. Try natural remedies for minor ailments, such as coconut oil for thrush and applied to your skin to prevent stretch marks, and ginger for nausea.
5. Wear secondhand maternity clothes.

The answer is to keep some perspective. It would be impossible to prevent exposure to every single man-made substance or chemical for nine long months – including car fumes, air pollution, chlorine at the pool and the cleaning products used in the studio where you do pregnancy yoga. Have you ever heard a mother saying 'Well, he's behind on his milestones because I painted my toenails when I was pregnant'? The truth is our bodies are remarkable at filtering out toxins and chemicals to protect our babies, and our babies are incredibly tenacious. As long as you follow the fairly straightforward guidelines from your doctor, your baby should be fine.

A sensible bit of advice is to avoid exposure to anything you find unpleasant. If the paint you are using is a bit whiffy, stop painting. If the petrol fumes really bug you, ask someone else to fill up the car. If a particular fabric or shower gel is making you itchy, avoid it. Trust your own judgement.

Natural
baby

Most babies are simple creatures with straightforward needs.

Where you can, seek out natural materials, which will help you avoid bisphenol A (BPA). BPA is a synthetic hormone that makes plastic clear and shatterproof but it can leach out of the plastic. Its use is carefully regulated[1] but for items that will go in your child's mouth, choose a more eco-friendly option.

Eco-friendly dummies

Avoid silicon and select natural rubber, a sustainable material harvested from the rubber tree. Rubber may not last quite as long as silicon, so check carefully for splits or tears before each use.

Eco-friendly teethers

Aargh! The trauma of teething and all those disturbed nights just when you thought you were establishing a routine. Teething can seem like a cruel trick from Mother Nature, but the right teethers will help ease the pain and frustration. Look for natural rubber, wooden, organic cotton or compostable teethers such as those made from corn starch.

Some people swear by amber teething necklaces, others view them as a hippie trend. The theory is that they contain succinic acid which can provide natural pain relief and has anti-inflammatory properties. Realistically the body is unlikely to absorb any succinic acid from the beads and its pain relief options are not proven. Anecdotal reviews vary, but do remove before sleeping due to the risk of choking or strangulation.

Carrying your baby in a sling or carrier is perfect for their first wild adventures

Baby-wearing

Baby-wearing – that is, carrying your baby in a sling – has become trendy in recent years but has been going on for centuries. Buggies have their place but can be a pain to manoeuvre in tight spaces, to get on and off public transport and on rough ground or sand (whatever the manufacturers may claim).

A sling, by contrast, lets you go anywhere and keeps your hands free so you can still hold hands with your eldest. Not only that, but your baby will generally be happier closer to you, lulled by your heartbeat and motion. Baby-wearing can also help prevent and manage colic.

You can go anywhere without being fazed by steps, escalators, mud or snow, and even breastfeed on the go! It's also the closest a father will get to experiencing pregnancy, with all its posture-challenging wonder

As your little one gets heavier, you'll need a back-carrier version. These are useful to give tired legs a rest even when your child starts walking. They can cost more than front carriers (although some front carriers are adaptable) but are easily found secondhand.

All about
reusables

Or how to succeed where I failed

There are two types of reusable nappy, the all-in-one where the inner nappy and waterproof outer are fixed together, and two-part nappies where they are separate. The all-in-one is more convenient but is more likely to leak and takes longer to dry.

Whatever style you use, you will be making a small saving in terms of carbon usage but a massive reduction in the non-biodegradable waste heading to landfill.

Recipe for a happy cloth bum

You will need:

20 inner nappies and 4 wraps, or 15 all-in-one nappies

disposable nappy liners (ensure they are biodegradable and flushable). Or select reusable fleece liners.

3 or 4 booster pads for extra night-time absorption

bucket with lid

eco detergent or soapnut shells

drying rack, line or tumble dryer

Take one baby and apply nappy, including wrap if required. Change nappy in case of poo or at least every three hours. Place nappy in bucket and flush liner. Clean baby's bum and apply a new nappy or have some bare botty time.

Wash nappies every three days or as required using an eco-detergent or the wonderful soapnut shells. Dry outside for extra brightness, but there may be occasions when you need to resort to the tumble dryer (if you have one).

The truth about reusable nappies

Sometimes a green zealot is so keen to convert you to reusables that you can feel the reality is somewhat glossed over in an (admirable) attempt to show you how wonderful it can be. There are a few facts which cannot be ignored.

Reusables are more work

It would be pointless to deny this. You will need a system for washing and drying them that will take more time than plonking a disposable in the bin. However, you are probably doing a wash a day anyway … so what's a couple more washes a week?

They will increase your electricity bill

Running your washing machine a couple of times extra a week will slightly increase your energy bill but you can minimize this by only running full loads. If you use a tumble dryer it can have a significant impact on your expenditure, but you are still likely to save money overall compared with using disposables. Compare how wasteful it would be if you bought new clothes every time they got dirty, rather than washing them.

A happy cloth botty

Top 10 reasons to ...
give reusables a go

1. No stinky nappy bins – and your landfill bin will thank you too if you are on fortnightly collection. Ever seen maggots wriggling out of an old disposable stuck to the bottom of the bin? Truly yuck.
2. Helps to prepare your child for potty training, as they can literally feel more in a reusable.
3. One-size options will see you through from newborn to potty training.
4. Good for twins (your bin would be overflowing otherwise).
5. Often better containment in the leg area (need I say more?).
6. No chemicals next to your baby's skin.
7. They won't explode weird wee-soaked gel if you chuck them downstairs (or at your partner). Absolute hell to tidy up!
8. Colourful or patterned wraps look lovely.
9. No landfill guilt for you.
10. You can buy them secondhand and save even more money, but do research the brands on offer first.

They will cost more upfront

Yes, they will. But invest in new nappies once and you will be better off overall, as they will last longer. To save money upfront, look out for schemes with your local council. Also, you will be showered with more newborn Babygros than the average baby could ever use. Try suggesting to friends and family that you would like a reusable nappy as a present instead.

Drying can be a nightmare

Lots of wet nappies on radiators or clothes horses create damp, unhealthy air. For those dreary days when you can't dry outside, limit indoor drying to a couple of rooms, such as the bathroom, and turn the extractor fan on or open the window a crack.

Reusable nappies don't like...

- being boiled
- fabric conditioner – it will leave a residue and make them less absorbent
- thick nappy cream
- bleach
- being left dirty for more than a few days.

Reusable nappies do like...

- being line-dried to brighten them naturally – watch the UV make those stains vanish!
- soapnut shells instead of detergent
- nappy liners
- being soaked prior to washing
- being changed frequently – don't leave a wet nappy on your baby.

Green [CHALLENGE] #12

You can avoid disposables at the pool by buying a special fabric swim nappy – make sure the leg and waist fit is super-snug to contain any incidents. It's worth taking two just in case.

Travelling with reusables

If you are off on holiday, to visit family or even camping, reverting to disposables can seem like the only option, but it is possible to make reusables work on the go:

- Stay in places with a washing machine or a laundry service.
- Use hybrid nappies where you have a disposable insert for travelling and wipe or rinse the rest.
- Invest in a waterproof wet/dry bag where you store your clean nappies in one side and your dirties in the other.
- To save space, prefolds with reusable covers take up less room than all-in-ones.
- If you are flying, you may find it hard to take your entire supply of nappies. Instead, take a few and wash frequently, by hand if necessary – easier if you are in self-catering accommodation.

What to do if you really don't get on with reusables?

As you know, I didn't manage it. Life isn't perfect, so whether it is because your child's carer isn't keen on reusables, there is family illness or you have only a few months left before you potty train, read on for the how-to-succeed-if-you've-failed guide!

Try half and half

The compromise option. Buy five or so reusable nappies and use them when convenient. You'll need to make yourself some rules to ensure you do bother with them (those disposables always seem to whisper 'use me, I'm so easy'). Try the first nappy change of the day, or perhaps a reusable for any nappy change at home.

You can also buy reusable outer nappies with just a disposable insert. This reduces the amount going to landfill and some inserts may compost successfully too.

Opt for eco-friendly disposables

Eco-friendly disposables are slightly more sustainable than regular disposable nappies but they are a lot more expensive.

Shop around for those that are free from chlorine bleaching, fragrance and latex, but you will not escape synthetic materials altogether. Even if they claim to be biodegradable, part of an eco-friendly disposable nappy will still outlive your great, great, great, great, great grandchildren. Sorry!

Consider elimination communication

Now I thought this was a bit 'out there' until I saw real-life people doing it. Basically, it involves responding to your baby's cues and popping them on a potty when they need to go. Some people even ditch the whole nappy thing altogether.

It has been argued that this method trains the parent, not the child. Either way, it leads to earlier potty training and fewer nappies used … but you will need to be a routine-driven person with the time to fully focus on your child and to have the patience of a saint. Cream carpets are not ideal either.

Is it Green or Gross… to reuse a disposable swim nappy several times? If there's no poo, just give it a rinse and dry on the line!

Super-soft, super-easy no-sew wipes

Baby
wipes

So you've sorted the nappy situation (whether that is reusable or disposable, I'm not judging!) but what about the wipes you use? All those plastic-packed, non-flushable and non-compostable wipes use a lot of resources. They can be very convenient for on the move, but for home why not make your own wipes?

If you are whizzy with the sewing machine, you can knock out proper stitched reusable wipes, but for the rest of us, these no-sew cloth wipes are the business.

Make your own no-sew cloth wipes

You will need 100% cotton fabric (soft flannel works particularly well) and pinking shears (so your fabric won't fray):

- Hot-wash the fabric to pre-shrink. When dry, simply cut with the pinking shears to your perfect wipe size.
- To use, either wet or make a gentle cleansing fluid by combining a dash of liquid baby soap with water and a few drops of olive oil. This works well if it is stored in a spray bottle for moistening.
- Soak your used wipes in a nappy bin before washing (twice a week should be fine).

For disposable wipes, look for ones containing water only. You don't need fragrance or other additives.

Is it Green or Gross...

to wipe your kid's bogeys/dribble on their T-shirt?
Saves on wipes, right?

Green bath
time

Bath time is my favourite time of the day, both my own (scorching hot with a book) or the children's (usually splashy and active, but sometimes calm and reflective). It provides a pre-bed ritual that not only cleanses but prepares the body for sleep. It's a chance to chat about the day with the children as well as check their bodies are healthy.

How do you make sure it is a natural and eco-friendly end to the day?

Too much too soon

There is no need to bath a baby every day: they're not exactly covered in mud (yet!), and too much washing can dry their skin. A quick wipe over and a little olive or coconut oil massage will keep their skin fresh and moisturized.

When your baby is a little older, bath time can be lots of fun. Hop in with your child (you are so much nicer than a plastic bath seat) and enjoy some skin on skin while getting clean together. In fact, the whole family can be bathed in one tub of water – start with the kids, then the adults (top up with a little hot) then let the dog go in last.

As your child gets a little older, a shower can be an enjoyable new experience and saves water too. My daughter insists on wearing her goggles in the shower so water doesn't go in her eyes.

Keep it natural and sustainable

All you need is a simple organic body wash that can be used on hair and skin. Opt for a short, natural ingredient list and you should be on to a winner.

Bath time can be splashy!

Natural products containing chamomile or lavender can make for a peaceful bath time

Avoiding products containing palm oil means you are not contributing to the destruction of the rainforest. Palm oil is grown in monocultures, resulting in the razing of wildlife-rich forests, particularly in South-East Asia. You may need to do a little research too, as often palm oil is listed as the innocent-sounding 'vegetable oil'.

Kill the duck

OK, don't actually kill it; that would be a bit traumatic. The rubber duck is usually made from plastic, sneaking more carbon into our lives.

If you do want to use plastic bath toys (and they are pretty good for squirting at Granny), select those without BPAs and phthalates, as they will inevitably end up in mouths. After a couple of months, your bath squirters will fill up with what is commonly known as Black Yucky Gunky Mouldy Stuff. Soaking them in vinegar will help to clean them.

Cuddle time

Is there anything sweeter than that after-bath cuddle in a soft towel? An organic and Fairtrade towel is worth investing in. A hood is a must, and buy larger than your baby needs. A good towel should last their childhood. Don't rush to let the bath water out either. While it is still warm it is heating the room, and it's a good chance to water the house plants.

And finally, why not try a biodegradable bamboo toothbrush rather than the usual plastic kind?

Recipe Make a natural bath bomb

For fabulous bath-time fun (and baby-soft skin afterwards, whatever your age), try this recipe. Your children can help make the bath bombs too.

Makes approximately 20 small Coco-baby Bath Bombs, depending on their size.

You will need:

2 tbsp Epsom salts

300g baking soda

150g citric acid (from your local chemist or online)

150g cornflour

2 tbsp of coconut oil

a little water (or cold herbal tea – chamomile works well)

moulds – try Play-Doh moulds, those used for making chocolates or experiment with household objects, such as a halved tennis ball or ice-cube trays

essential oils or natural food colouring (both optional)

Simply mix the salts, baking soda, citric acid and cornflour together. Now add in the coconut oil and combine with your hands until it is sandy in texture (a bit like rubbing butter into a crumble mixture). Do be careful that it doesn't get in eyes or mouth.

Add a few drops of essential oils or colouring to your water (or cold tea), then add it very cautiously – a teaspoon at a time – to the salts mixture. Combine well and expect a little fizz! You hardly need to add any liquid until it is like slightly damp, perfect-sandcastle sand, which forms a lump when squeezed together.

Squeeze into your moulds and leave overnight to dry, away from moisture or direct heat. Store in an airtight container and pop one in the bath for fizzy fun. A bath mat is a good idea, as the coconut oil can make everything (child included) a bit slippery!

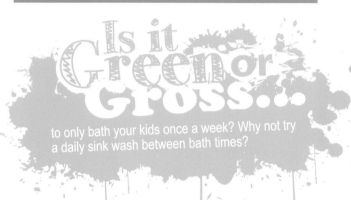

Is it Green or Gross... to only bath your kids once a week? Why not try a daily sink wash between bath times?

Green [CHALLENGE] #13

During a heatwave, try using a long garden hose to syphon the bath water out of the bathroom window into a container in the garden. Here's how:

1. Stick the garden hose out of the window (the neighbours will think you are insane) and weigh the other end down in the bath.
2. Go outside. If you have amazing suction power, you can suck on the end of the hose until water flows. Gravity will ensure the bath empties.
3. Alternatively, try a syphon pump.
4. Use the water within a few days (except on any plants you plan to eat!).

Mindful
moments

Body and mind are so interlinked – neither can feel truly healthy and balanced without the other being so too. Nature and time outdoors are good for both.

If you've got something to talk about with your child, such as feedback from school or worries they may have, taking a potentially difficult conversation outdoors can be really helpful. Your child may release their frustrations or access their feelings more easily by walking while talking.

The outdoors is also a brilliant place for learning about mindfulness, the practice of living in the moment. Young children are innate experts at mindful behaviour, but as they grow older they need to relearn this valuable practice.

Time to just be

Top 5 ways to ... learn mindfulness together

1. Allow an insect to crawl on your arm, feel the light tickle on your skin and admire its colours.

2. Teach a young child to become aware of their breathing. Lie down together with a cuddly teddy and explain that you are going to soothe the teddy to sleep by breathing deeply so your tummy moves up and down. Try and breathe in through the nose and out through the mouth.

3. Ask your child to shut their eyes or wear a blindfold and give them different foods to taste and guess what they are. Use foods that they enjoy or that will surprise them, such as an ice cube or popping candy.

4. Try to pause during everyday life. How about taking three deep breaths together before opening the front door to leave for school or nursery each morning?

5. Learn to listen. Sit somewhere, ideally outside, without talking for a few minutes. Draw a picture of, or write down, anything you can hear, whether that is birdsong, planes or sirens.

Urban **jungle**

One of the biggest issues for urban health is air pollution. The air quality in most cities worldwide (that monitor outdoor air pollution) is failing to meet World Health Organization guidelines for safe levels. The risk is respiratory disease and other health problems.[2]

If your child suffers from asthma or other respiratory disorders it is sensible to check air pollution levels (available online or in the newspaper for major cities) before playing outside for prolonged periods. The further you can get from the traffic the better, so once again, those brilliant urban parks are perfect for a safe outdoors adventure.

Natural remedies that are worth a go

Natural alternatives for **minor ailments**

Conventional medicine can be vital, but for minor ills it is worth trying the natural approach first. You can always resort to the doctor or chemist if you don't see an improvement.

Insect bites

Prevent bites with a few drops of citronella or lavender oil topically applied in a light carrier oil (olive or almond are ideal). Try 15 drops of essential oil to 100ml of carrier oil for an effective blend. This is best applied and rubbed in before getting dressed.

Or, for a spray that is easier to use on the go, try this recipe.

You will need:
- spray bottle
- boiled water
- witch hazel (to fill half your spray bottle)
- any of these essential oils, or use a few together: citronella, teatree, eucalyptus, lavender or rosemary

Half fill a spray bottle with cooled, boiled water, then add witch hazel almost to the top.

Now add in 20 drops of essential oils for every 100ml of fluid in your bottle.

Use within two months. It can be kept in the fridge for a refreshing tingle on hot days.

If the bugs do bite, lavender or tea-tree oil or a calendula-based cream will relieve itching.

Chicken pox

If your child is old enough, give them a little pot of soothing cornflour (corn starch) to apply to their spots when they itch. At bath time, try a sock full of porridge oats placed under the hot tap when running. It will release a creamy white liquid that is very calming for irritated skin. A good handful of bicarbonate of soda in the bath is another popular and effective remedy.

Bruises

A pack of frozen peas wrapped in a towel used as a cold compress will help reduce swelling and pain.

A little arnica gel (made from a plant in the daisy family) is beneficial for bruises and sprains.

Minor cuts and grazes

First, make sure the broken skin is cleaned with fresh water. Dilute a few drops of tea-tree oil in water and use as an antibacterial rinse. A little air time will dry it naturally and then soothe with calendula cream.

Travel sickness

Simple bands that activate pressure points on the wrist can help relieve travel sickness without medication. Children's sizes are available. Alternatively, herbal remedies can be purchased.

Constipation

Check your child's diet and see if foods such as bananas or white bread are causing problems, avoiding them if so. Then introduce the Ps to poo ... that is, certain foods beginning with 'P' that can have a laxative effect, such as prunes, peas, peaches, pears and plums (apricots are good as well).

Linseeds are a magical ingredient for bowel action. Bake them into crumble toppings, bread or muffins for hidden results. Drinking plenty of fluids is essential too.

A tummy massage can soothe and encourage a bowel movement and works well in a warm bath. Start at the navel and massage in a clockwise direction. A little cycling in the air can get things moving – just lay your baby on their back and move their legs as if they are riding a bike.

Eczema

Fish-oil supplements can help improve eczema, and if you are trying to avoid steroid creams, then try a topical application of aloe vera in the morning and coconut oil in the evening for a powerful combination of soothing, moisturizing and antibacterial properties.

Cradle cap

A crusty scalp can be eradicated without resorting to an anti-dandruff shampoo. Coconut oil is magical stuff here, as it is works without being as greasy as olive oil, and it has antifungal properties (occasionally a cradle cap outbreak is caused by fungus).

Green [CHALLENGE] #14

Stock the medicine cupboard with natural alternatives: arnica gel, calendula cream and tea-tree oil make a great start, as already mentioned.

Also try natural witch hazel, a powerful astringent that when applied on cotton wool can reduce bruising and stop minor cuts bleeding. It is good for teething infants: mix a teaspoon of witch-hazel tea with one drop of clove and myrrh oil and rub on the affected area. It can help you too – witch hazel on cotton-wool pads can reduce dark circles under the eyes.

Aloe vera works really well for treating sunburn, insect bites or itchy rashes. Freeze the gel in an ice-cube tray, and simply pop out a soothing, cooling cube when needed.

Coconut oil is naturally antibacterial and antifungal so is perfect for treating thrush and athlete's foot. As it is very moisturizing and increases the lipid content of the skin, it can help dry skin and eczema. It is also delicious and healthy as a vegan substitute for butter in cooking and can even be used as a natural underarm deodorant.

Raw honey is another powerful medicine. It is full of enzymes and antioxidants, with antibacterial properties. Use it on burns and minor cuts to speed the healing process and keep them infection-free. It is great for colds in a honey and lemon tea or taken by the spoonful for a cough. Consume in moderation and don't forget that babies under 12 months old shouldn't eat honey. Look for one labelled 10+ for it to work effectively, but don't feel you have to spend money on manuka.

Finally, mullein oil is useful for ear pain. Just a few drops into the affected ear twice a day should help and can be used in conjunction with antibiotics.

Just massage it on to the scalp before bath time, and leave to soak in for a few minutes. Then take a very soft nail brush and gently remove as much of the brown crustiness as you can. Gently is the key and you don't have to do it all in one go – make sure your baby is happy, and don't break the skin. Then wash your baby's hair with a natural shampoo and towel dry. Next, reapply a little coconut oil to leave on.

Repeat for a few days and that crustiness should be gone. Coconut oil is so lovely for skin that it is a good habit to regularly oil your baby after the bath anyway.

Head lice

Nothing will clear a hairdresser's quicker than a cry of 'nits!'. Keep on top of an infestation with regular checks of your child's hair and scalp so that you spot any little visitors before the frantic head-itching stage. Look behind the ears and the nape of the neck for the brownish-grey insects that are about the size of a sesame seed.

If you do spot any nits, use a fine-toothed nit comb for wet-combing in the bath. Couple this with a suffocation technique (stopping the lice from breathing by applying olive oil or a thick hair conditioner, ideally with a drop of tea-tree oil in it) and you'll soon be nit-free. Afterwards, clean the comb by soaking it in vinegar for half an hour.

You will need to treat the whole family together and repeat this daily for a week. Recheck everyone on a weekly basis and use a tea-tree oil conditioner to help prevent another infestation. This may sound like lots of hassle, but it is worth knowing that chemical treatments are becoming less effective as head lice develop resistance to them.

During and after antibiotics

Sometimes, there is no substitute for antibiotics and make sure you finish the course to avoid future resistance. Because antibiotics upset the natural balance of the gut, it is a good idea to eat live yoghurt during and after the course to help the digestive system return to normal.

Prevent sunburn

A little time in the sun, unprotected, is necessary for the body to make vitamin D so the bones can absorb calcium. Many children, with their indoor lifestyles and overzealous parents whacking on the sun cream, are deficient in this vital vitamin.[3] Allow your children some SPF-free time (up to 15 minutes is usually about right), but keep a close eye on their delicate skin. The ingredients in sun block (usually titanium dioxide or zinc oxide) are bad for marine life, as a chemical reaction can harm the microscopic algae that feed everything from small fish to whales.[4] Ensuring your child wears a sun suit (and hence minimizing the amount of cream needed before a dip in the sea) will help.

You can make your own quick and natural sun cream (roughly SPF20 – add more zinc to give higher protection). This zinc-oxide-based lotion will sit on top of the skin rather than be absorbed by it.

You will need:

- 250ml of your favourite body lotion (make sure it doesn't contain citrus oils, as they can increase the skin's sensitivity to sunlight)
- 2 tbsp zinc-oxide powder (this can be bought online, but make sure it is non-nano, non-micronized – a nano particle will enter the bloodstream but a non-nano will not)

Pour the lotion in a bowl and whisk in the zinc-oxide powder until smooth. Then pour back in to the bottle (you'll have a little extra too).

This sun cream provides instant protection but isn't waterproof, so reapply after swimming or sweaty exercise.

Disposal of unused medicines

The first priority when disposing of unwanted medicines is, of course, the safety of your children, but pouring them down the sink just puts them back into our environment.

It's best to drop them at a take-back scheme: your doctor's surgery may run one. The outdoor wheelie bin is the next best option.

Your
body

There's all this talk of how to keep your child healthy, but what about you? Being a parent makes you acutely aware that you will not live for ever (it is fair to say that you will biodegrade faster than a disposable nappy!). It is often the wake-up call that you are suddenly very necessary for the well-being of your child. Unfortunately, the birth of a child also removes the luxury of time. You may put sun cream and a hat on your babe but forget yourself; you will have less opportunity to exercise and more inclination to self-medicate with alcohol or chocolate of an evening. Then there is the baby weight and stretched tummy, and that

Build exercise into family life

applies whether you are the mother or father – many a sympathy pound has been gained by knackered dads to survive the day at work.

Not only that, but many parents have double caring roles, both for their young children and elderly or disabled relatives. Known as the 'sandwich generation', there are 2.4 million people in the UK who find themselves in that situation.[5] Carving out a little time to take care of yourself in those circumstances may feel impossible, but it is vital.

The fact is, looking after yourself is as much your duty as looking after your child. Self-care should be top of your agenda: you simply cannot look after someone properly if you are not looking after yourself. Try to eat food that you would be happy to feed your child, and avoid the temptation to skip meals to save extra cooking. Sitting down with your children to eat is an important part of family life.

Building exercise into your life will help you regulate stress and stay healthy. Walking every day is the best start to achieving this. Healthy, active parents are far more likely to end up with healthy, active kids. It's also about focusing on the long term – yes, you want to be fit enough to push your children on the swing for half an hour, but how about being able to do that for your grandchildren too?

Footnotes for Chapter 5

1 European Food Safety Agency (2015). 'Bisphenol A'. http://www.efsa.europa.eu/en/topics/topic/bisphenol.htm

2 World Health Organization (2014). 'Ambient (outdoor) air pollution in cities database'. http://www.who.int/phe/health_topics/outdoorair/databases/cities/en/.

3 Pacaud, M. M. et al. (2008). 'Vitamin D deficiency in children and its management: review of current knowledge and recommendations'. *Pediatrics* 122: 398-417.

4 Tovar-Sanchez, A. et al. (2014). 'Sunscreens as a source of hydrogen peroxide production in coastal waters' *Environmental Science & Technology 48(16): 9037-42.*

5 Drakakis, H. (2013). 'Carer-friendly policies needed to relieve pressure on the "sandwich generation"'. http://www.theguardian.com/society/2013/oct/25/carer-friendly-policies-sandwich-generation

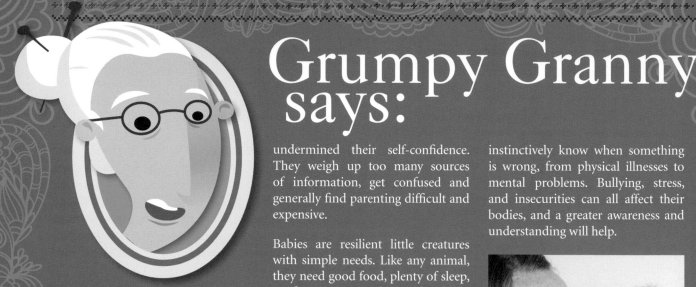

Grumpy Granny says:

Time to relax

Why can't intelligent, sensible, capable people learn to trust themselves? The current parenting generation are meant to be the best educated so far, but they exhibit a high level of incompetence when it comes to using common sense.

My grandchildren are being brought up in different ways, with approaches ranging from structured routines to child-centred. But there is a common characteristic in that their parents struggle to have faith in themselves and their instincts.

If these same people were looking after a new puppy or kitten, they would know what to do to keep it safe. They would automatically make the right decisions in most everyday situations. But when it comes to their own offspring, the internet has undermined their self-confidence. They weigh up too many sources of information, get confused and generally find parenting difficult and expensive.

Babies are resilient little creatures with simple needs. Like any animal, they need good food, plenty of sleep, a safe environment, love and cuddles. They do not need special creams and lotions; they usually have wonderful skin that looks after itself. Electric, plug-in video sleep monitors are unnecessary if you are in the same house as the baby – they have lungs and loud cries that will successfully wake a sleeping household. Even thermometers are not really needed, as it will soon become obvious by touch if a child has a high temperature.

The environment suffers when parents treat their kids as a project. Running to the internet for advice can trick them into buying an even greater range of consumer items to cure non-existent problems. Many sites that appear independent are often used as marketing opportunities by commercial companies.

A better way of looking after children is to learn from them. Discover what is normal for them, then you will instinctively know when something is wrong, from physical illnesses to mental problems. Bullying, stress, and insecurities can all affect their bodies, and a greater awareness and understanding will help.

You need to trust your own instincts as a parent

To protect their health and well-being, get them outside, get them exercising and become a sounding board for their worries. Learn to listen without always telling them what to do, and they should open up to you.

Little green fingers

6

How can you make your garden better for wildlife?

In my life before children, I didn't have much time for gardening. The lawn had a trim when I remembered, the shrubs – whose names I didn't know or care about – got a yearly prune, and then I was off out, thank you very much.

When my children came along, two things changed. Firstly, it became much harder to just go out (there are only so many babysitting favours you can call in), so unless I wanted to sit around on the sofa or do housework, I needed to find other interests around the home. Soon, 'getting out' evolved to mean 'time in the garden'. Secondly, I realized that my children had an innate interest in gardening. They love to dig, discover worms and watch the seeds they have sown grow into food for us. They like to know their patch and to be proud of what they have achieved.

Gardening teaches children a lot: the obvious educational stuff, such as the names of plants and processes such as photosynthesis, but also real-life skills. They will learn when to be gentle (transferring a seedling) and when to be firm (digging hard ground). They will have to be patient, as gardening is rarely instant gratification, and alongside that they will experience the sweet taste of success (of the season's first strawberry) and the sad disappointment of failure (we forgot to water the sunflowers). Not only that, it's good exercise and stress relief for all the family too. No wonder gardening is popular with all age groups.

Most importantly, a garden can be buzzing, flitting and humming with wonderful wildlife. Taking action for the creatures that share our gardens is a vital part of being a green family. In fact, gardens make up a significant proportion of outdoor space, offering homes for wildlife as well as acting as green corridors that allow animals to move around the wider countryside. This chapter will help you create a space for nature where your children can be involved. It needs to be a safe, interactive, hands-on haven. It should be low-maintenance and easy to fit into busy family life. Whether your garden is the size of a postage stamp or requires a ride-on mower, a little outdoor space for children to discover nature is worth a lot. But if you don't have a garden, don't despair. With just a few simple projects, a balcony can offer plenty: you could even grow a mini wildflower meadow on your windowsill. Alternatively, you could think big, and consider an allotment for growing food, welcoming nature and family exercise.

Embracing a wild garden, hacking at plants a little less, using fewer chemicals, reducing how often you mow: all are perfect for a lazy gardener, and with the time you save, there are lovely activities that children, and the wildlife in your garden, will appreciate.

Holly blue butterfly

The ingredients for a family **wildlife garden**

You will need:

- space to play
- sensory plants
- snacks for kids
- dinner for wildlife
- wet stuff
- shelter
- natural alternatives to chemicals
- a messy corner

Space to **play**

However much or little space you have available, it is important to allow areas for the children to play without continually policing them.

The good old lawn is the first place to start. With a few changes you can make it a haven for wildlife as well as robust enough for games all year round.

I must first confess that I am not one of the stripy-lawn brigade. I do admire owners of a perfect lawn, but in much in the same way as I admire someone who irons their pants. While a lush green carpet looks nice, it is clearly not being played on enough or doing the job for wildlife.

Sowing the seeds of the future

The dandelion

The first step is to rethink the weed. Plants such as the dandelion, daisy, red and white clover, plantain, moss and black medic are considered weeds that many gardeners try to eradicate with chemicals. As our threatened bees buzz happily over these rich nectar and pollen sources, I find myself asking 'weeds to whom, exactly?'

You don't have to mow every week during the growing months, and when you do, leave some of the grass clippings in place because they contain

Green [CHALLENGE] #15

This will have stripy-lawn lovers quaking in their wellies, but it is only a temporary effect. To write a name or initial on the lawn, cut out the required letters in thick card or dark plastic and fix to the lawn using tent pegs or weigh them down with heavy stones. Leave them for a week, and then remove to expose the yellow name. The grass won't take long to return and it provides an interesting opportunity to chat about plants needing light in order to photosynthesize. This may help...

Photosynthesis revision class

Photosynthesis is how plants make their food. They need light, carbon dioxide and water to do it. They breathe in the carbon dioxide and suck up water through their roots. Then it is over to the chloroplasts (responsible for the green colour in leaves) which turn the water, carbon dioxide and light into sugar (food) and oxygen. When there is no light, the chloroplasts stop making the green colour, but when the light comes back, they start again.

the same nutrients as fertilizer, including nitrogen, phosphorus and potassium. Your garden will thrive naturally. Consider allowing areas of long grass too, perhaps even mowing a path through it. You could add to the interest by planting wildflower plugs in autumn to create a wildflower meadow (of any size). Annual meadows will have to be reseeded yearly, or will reseed themselves (annual plants include poppies, cornflowers, corncockle and marigold) whereas a perennial meadow (including plants such as oxeye daisies, scabious, geranium and plantain) will regrow from root each year. Make sure you mow after flowering (early autumn) so that it has a chance to produce seeds, and then remove any cuttings to avoid smothering the plants.

Stepping stones

Flower beds and vegetable patches don't have to be out of bounds. Adding stepping stones or pathways turns them into jungle adventure zones and encourages exploration while protecting your plants.

Plant some sunflowers

Hedge benefits

Hedges are great for nesting birds (don't cut them until the breeding season has finished in September) but they can also have hidden adventure opportunities. Many mature hedges, particularly evergreen species such as laurel, have secret tunnels inside (more likely if they are next to a fence) that with some light pruning can be made accessible to little people. But 1) beware of eye-height pokey sticks and 2) it is really hard to lure your child out of a hedge tunnel.

Snacks for kids

Having sweet and yummy treats that you can just pick off the bush is fun for children. They will often eat fruit like cherry tomatoes off the plant but if you put them on their plate they can get left.

Keep plants accessible, on the patio or near the back door, for easy munching.

Try strawberries in planters (big containers with holes in the sides) or blueberries in pots (if you just want one plant, check it is self-pollinating).

A growbag is an easy way to grow cherry tomatoes, peas or cucumbers. Once the risk of frost has passed in early spring, place your bag in full sunlight and poke a few drainage holes in the bottom. Cucumbers and tomatoes will like the bag horizontal; for peas, pop it upright. Cut out holes for your plants and add some canes for support. Remember to water and feed regularly.

Sensory **plants**

Part of the wonder of gardens is the range of textures and scents. If you have a wide variety of plants, you are more likely to attract a wide variety of different birds too.

Top 5 ... sensory delights in the garden

1. Herbs such as rosemary, parsley and thyme are easy to grow from seed and are great for a game of 'which herb?' where children have to guess the herb using only smell and taste. They grow well in a window box or inside on a bright windowsill.

2. Furry soft leaves such as the gorgeous lamb's ear are popular with children. Also try dusty miller: its prettily shaped, light-grey leaves are woolly and fuzzy.

3. Plants with popular scents include lavender and jasmine, but sweet peas and honeysuckle are also beautifully fragrant.

4. Introduce interesting shapes into the garden. The branches of the corkscrew hazel form a twisted pattern, offer long yellow catkins to play with and edible nuts too. The branches are often used in flower arranging, if you are feeling creative.

5. Don't rule out prickles. Learning how to touch a holly bush or mahonia is part of life; just avoid children playing barefoot near these bushes where fallen leaves can be painful. These prickly plants' berries are often vital for the survival of birds in winter.

Native berries such as hawthorns will help birds survive the winter

Dinner for **wildlife**

Part of being a good host is laying on plenty of good food, whether you are visited by friends (cake and coffee) or birds and insects (seeds, berries and nectar).

When people think of feeding wildlife, the mind often springs to bird feeders full of peanuts, but human-assisted offerings fail when you go on holiday or forget. Thoughtful planting and gardening will ensure a plentiful supply of food that will enable wildlife to help themselves for most of the year.

Berry nice

Ensuring a good supply of winter berries is a brilliant way of helping birds get through the coldest months. Cotoneaster, hawthorn, rowan, holly and ivy are good options. Amazingly, weight for weight, the dry pith of ivy berries can contain nearly as many calories as a Mars bar[1] (but are poisonous for humans so ensure your ivy is out of reach of toddlers).

*The beautiful teasel –
a goldfinch restaurant*

Bee fun

One of the most important things you can do to help our declining bee species is to plant nectar-rich plants. Try the beautiful catmint, hyssop, marjoram or wood sage 'May Night'. Butterflies will especially love buddleia and lavender. The stunning purple phacelia is another nectar-rich beauty.

It really helps to prolong flowering if you deadhead regularly and keep your plants well watered, as hydrated plants will make more nectar.

Seedy is good

Planting a bird food border is a colourful way of providing seeds. The sculptural teasel is packed full of tiny seeds that goldfinches love, and sparkling with frost it makes a beautiful addition to an otherwise sparse winter garden. Lavender, sunflowers, wheat and mustard will also provide nutritious seeds for birds – just leave them in place when flowering is over.

For a quick fix, you can even sow the bird seed you'd normally put in your feeders. Unless it's been heat-treated to stop it germinating (manufacturers will state this on the bag), it should grow.

*The gorgeous tortoiseshell
butterfly seeking nectar*

Keep that bird table topped up

Mind the gap

There is a particular time when your help is vital. The hungry gap (no, not the hour before dinner) is the time of year when last year's seeds, nuts and berries have all gone, but spring has not yet brought other food opportunities. This is when it is particularly important to top up the bird feeder and make sure the bird table is full.

For the best feeding station you will need:

- 1 filled nyjer seed feeder (tiny black seeds that goldfinches adore)
- a feeder with mixed seeds (black sunflower seeds are popular). Avoid mixes packed full of fillers such as wheat, barley or lentils
- a well-stocked bird table (see below)
- fat balls, particularly for the winter months – make your own but if buying, never serve them in the mesh bag as this can trap little birdie feet
- fruit, such as apples and bananas. Feed these on the ground or the bird table, or try an apple feeder

For bird tables a mixed seed blend is ideal, but carefully selected leftovers can be left too. Don't put out mouldy food. Leftovers that are OK for birds:

- mild grated Cheddar
- leftover mild Cheddar sandwiches
- fruit, such as apples or bananas: cut out any bad bits if they are past their best to avoid mould
- rice (with no added salt).

Putting food out for birds comes with certain responsibilities. You will need to clean feeders and tables in a mild disinfectant every fortnight to make it less likely that disease will spread between birds. It can help to move your feeding station to a new area every month if possible.

Make sure food isn't left on the ground after nightfall, as this could attract rats or foxes. Also remove any uneaten scraps from bird tables after a few days.

Easy-peasy fat balls

I've made this recipe with the help of hundreds of children at various nature events over the years. Literally thousands of birds have enjoyed the results and now yours can too.

Add a block of room-temperature lard (warm until it is soft) to 2 mugs full of any combination of the following: dried fruit, oats, crushed nuts, seeds or grated mild Cheddar cheese.

Mix it together, getting very sticky paws in the process, and put into containers such as empty yogurt pots (with string tied into a hole in the base). Or just form ball shapes to go on the bird table. Leave them to set hard in the fridge before hanging out. They will store happily in the fridge for a few weeks, or if you make lots you can freeze some for later.

Apples are popular with birds

Is it Green or Gross...

to feed the birds live mealworms? Just get them delivered in the post – the robins will love it and so will the children.

Wet
stuff

Water is the stuff of life, but when you have children it is easy to see only the risks. Deep ponds are sensibly filled in, but often no replacement is considered.

A garden without a pond is a garden without … frogspawn, water snails, pond skaters, dragonfly larvae, newts and so much more. All these creatures are fascinating to children. There are simple, attractive and safe alternatives that will provide the much-needed habitat, drinking and bathing opportunities for wildlife, without the worry for you.

Birdie bath time

A bird bath can make an attractive focal point and it is lovely to watch blackbirds and starlings having a splash. Choose your style carefully because many feature a concrete top section resting precariously on a stand. This could easily be pulled over by a curious toddler. Keep it topped up with fresh water and give it a weekly rinse out – birds are as indiscriminate as babies about pooing in the bath.

Alternatively, stack bricks with a shallow terracotta container on top or, even more simply, use a plant saucer with a stone placed in the middle.

Pond life

The trick is to keep your pond small for safety and ease of care. Any watertight container, such as an old sink, can be buried to soil height and become a mini pond. A wooden half-barrel with pond liner and water plants will be at toddler height for looking in. You will need small oxygenating varieties, such as the dwarf water lily. Many don't need planting – they just float.

A wooden ramp or pile of stones will help wildlife such as frogs to access the space and a few rocks nearby will offer a hiding place for amphibians.

Create a bog garden

If you don't want a pond, or are filling in an existing one, then consider an option that is far from bog standard. The bog garden is a way of introducing a new wildlife habitat and works particularly well if you have an area of ground that is lower than the rest. Plants which love damp soil are often the most stunning.

If you are replacing an old pond, first rehome any aquatic life, then simply pierce the liner and allow to drain for a day or two. Then put a layer of gravel on the liner and build up to just below ground level with soil. Now you are ready for planting.

If you are starting from scratch, follow these instructions:

You will need:

- string
- a spade and fork
- pond liner to your desired size
- a few bricks
- a leaky hose (optional)
- a few buckets full of gravel (depending on the size of your bog garden, 3 buckets should suffice for a 1m² area)

Firstly, mark out your chosen area with string. A metre squared would be a good starting size – you can always extend later. Now dig out the area to a depth of 50cm and keep the soil to one side.

Line with the pond liner and place bricks round the edge to hold it in place. Then pierce it with the fork, every 20cm or so.

You may wish to include a leaky hose for easy watering. If so place it in the bottom now, with the bog garden end blocked with an end plug (which can be purchased cheaply from a garden centre or DIY store) and the other end coming out of the pond so you can easily attach the hosepipe when watering is required.

Line the bottom with gravel (and cover the hose if using) to stop the holes becoming clogged with soil. Aim for 3cm (1") of gravel all over. Next, put the excavated soil back in. It will be higher than it was, but resist the urge to compact it down. Simply let it rest for a few days and it should settle. If it doesn't, remove 3-5cm (1-2") of soil.

Welcome the amphibians to your garden

Planting your bog garden

For ease, plant before the soil is wet. Try candelabra primulas, hostas in different colours, lilies and tiny water forget-me-nots. Look out for plants with Latin names that include *alustris* or *ulignosus*, which mean 'bog' and 'marsh'.

Gently position the plants without compacting the soil around their roots. Wet the area until saturated, ideally using rainwater. Depending on the weather and how damp the area is naturally, you may need to keep it watered at certain points in the year. Look out for frogs, toads and grass snakes, as well as dragonflies, damselflies, bees and butterflies.

Reduce your need for water

Being a sustainable gardener involves reducing your water use. A water butt is a must, and so is bothering to use it rather than resorting to the hose because you are in a rush.

You can minimize your need for water by planting drought-tolerant native plants. Look for ones with silver or grey-green leaves because they reflect the sun's rays, thus helping them to conserve water. They will only need watering while they are being established. Ask at your local garden centre for advice.

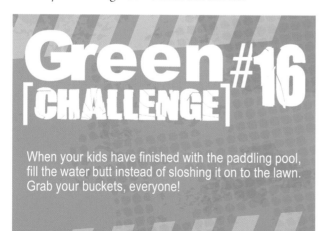

Green [CHALLENGE] #16

When your kids have finished with the paddling pool, fill the water butt instead of sloshing it on to the lawn. Grab your buckets, everyone!

Collect rainwater in a butt to water plants

Shelter

You've heard of a B&B. Well, this is all about accommodation for B&B&B&Bs: bats, birds, bugs and bees. And don't forget hedgehogs either.

Bat box

As houses get ever more maintained and old buildings are converted, bats are finding it hard to find places to roost.

Bat boxes look like bird boxes that someone forgot to put a hole in. This is because bats prefer a little hidden opening underneath. Do buy one made from untreated wood or look online for guides to make your own – they are easier to construct than bird boxes. Any sheltered spot in your garden will work for your box, ideally avoiding due south.

It is illegal to open a bat box once it is in place, unless you have a licence, as it could disturb this protected species. Once the box is up, it shouldn't require any maintenance.

Bird box

Even a tiny garden has room for a nest box. Try boxes with different-sized holes, to attract different species. For blue tits, 25mm is about right, whereas a starling would need 45mm. Robins and wrens favour a panel with an opening at the top.

Shelter and shade are important, so the side of a shed or in a tree, or even fixed to a wall or fence, is great. Make sure it is protected from the full glare of the sun. A clear flight path into the box is essential too.

You'll need to clean out the nest box between September and January to take out old nests and, sadly, any failed eggs or dead chicks. Sterilize the box with boiling water and allow to dry before rehanging. Make sure you and the children wash hands very thoroughly after cleaning out the boxes. Be aware that old nests can contain fleas so if you want to bring the nests inside, place them in a sealed bag in your freezer for 24 hours first.

Put up your bird box in early January, ready for the breeding season

A messy corner

Think of the messy drawers in your house. Spare batteries, random foreign coins, pens, string, scissors – the assorted flotsam and jetsam of life. Messy, yes, but also vital, not least for letting you keep everywhere else a bit tidier.

Ragged robin – weed or wonderful?

Nettles are not the enemy – they are great for wildlife

Don't forget to embrace the weed too. For example, stinging nettles are fabulous for butterflies and highly nutritious for you – see the nettle muffins recipe section in Chapter 4. Many so-called 'weeds' are very attractive and deserve a place in your flowerbeds – have a closer look at vetch, buttercups, ragged robin, cowslips, dandelions and scarlet pimpernel.

Your garden needs its messy space too. A small corner of wilderness where weeds can grow, sticks can rot and leaves can decompose. Celebrate its existence with a child-made sign saying 'nature reserve' or 'wild zone'.

Green [CHALLENGE] #17

For peat's sake, don't use peat. It is harvested from peat bogs, which are important ecosystems supporting rich biodiversity as well as storing carbon for us. Try making your own compost from fruit and veg peel and garden waste, or ensure you buy peat-free compost, which performs just as well.

A simple garden design that can be adapted depending on the size of your garden

Labels within the plan: Bird Food Border · Stepping Stones · Wild Flower Area · Bog Garden · ratio · Ivy Log · Tree · Nest Box · Tree · Mown Grass Circle · Small raised Bed · Pollen & Nectar Border · Playhouse · Shed

A plan for your family wildlife **garden**

The plan above includes many of the ideas discussed in this chapter. See page 134 for a suitable plan for a balcony, patio or small back yard.

Green #18
[CHALLENGE]

Find as many snails as you can and mark half of them on the shell with a little splodge of nail varnish and the other half with white correction fluid. Put them on separate sides of the garden, leave them for a few hours (or days), and then see which team gets to the other side of the garden first.

Urban jungle

What if your garden is miniature? Don't under-estimate what you can do with a tiny patio or even a balcony. Bird feeders can be attached directly to your windows and you can put up nest boxes just under eaves. The sociable little house sparrow or our summer visitors, house martins and swallows, will be glad of these.

Most options that work for bigger spaces can be scaled down. You may not have room for a wildflower meadow, but a miniature one is lovely too.

Make a mini-wildlife meadow for your balcony

You will need:

- a window box, seed tray or large pot
- peat-free compost, enough to fill your container
- mixed wildflower seeds (look for oxeye daisy, bird's-foot-trefoil, red clover, poppy, cornflower and greater knapweed for an attractive and nectar-rich blend). 3g (0.1oz) of seeds covers approximately 1m^2 (approx 3ft^2)

Autumn or early spring is the best time to sow your seeds.

Fill your container with the compost and pat down. Sprinkle over the seeds and lightly press them in (don't bury them). Now place in a sunny spot and water lightly. Keep moist and you should end up with a mini-meadow buzzing with bees by early summer.

Red campion

The beautiful poppy is stunning in a wildflower area

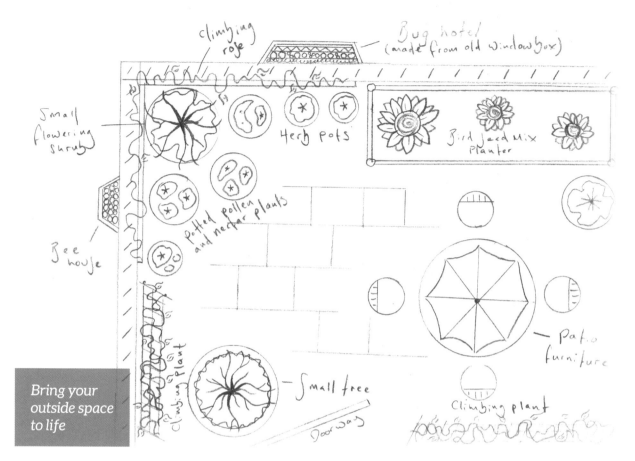

Bring your
outside space
to life

Labels in illustration:
climbing rose
Bug hotel (made from old window box)
Small flowering shrub
Herb pots
Bird Seed Mix Planter
Bee house
Potted pollen and nectar plants
Climbing Plant
Small tree
Doorway
Patio furniture
Climbing plant

A plan for your balcony or patio

This simple plan will bring fragrance and colour to your balcony or patio and a welcome space for nature in an urban area.

Invest in some large pots and fill them with a variety of plants. Try a pretty flowering shrub (for example, a hebe) and some nectar-rich plants, such as lavender, nasturtiums and marigolds. Herbs will be handy for cooking and bees will particularly welcome marjoram, rosemary, sage and thyme, all of which should grow happily in containers. Don't rule out trees either – a dwarf fruit tree or a bay will cope well in a pot, so long as you keep it well watered. A bee house and bug hotel could be on the outside of your balcony (as shown above) or inside a patio or back yard.

Window boxes will give you more space to grow, but don't just use them for plants – they make a great venue for a bug hotel too. Finally, add in some climbers to add interest, soften hard walls or fences and provide shelter for insects and birds. Ivy, honeysuckle or a climbing rose can be easily grown in pots against a trellis. And if you crave more space, there is always the option of an allotment.

Allotments

If you want to feed the family, but don't have the space for a decent vegetable patch at home, then the allotment is a winner.

Growing your own can save you money and gives you a cheap yet satisfying way to spend your weekends –

when you are digging the land you are not spending money on leisure activities.

Allotments are brilliant for the environment. They educate us about seasonal produce and help train us away from expecting strawberries all year round. They reduce the carbon footprint of our dinner and show us that wonky, five-legged carrots can taste as good (or better) than homogenized supermarket produce.

Many allotment sites, particularly in urban areas, have massive waiting lists. Some people hang on for several years before their dream comes true. Waiting lists for the most prestigious schools or super-cars are often not that long!

Taking on an allotment is a bit like having a new member of the family. It's a massive commitment, tiring at times, but highly rewarding. And once you are used to the routines, you won't be able to imagine life without it.

If you are lucky enough to gain an allotment plot, here are a few top tips to make it work for you and nature.

Top 5 tips for ... allotment success

1. You could share with a friend or only cultivate half the plot to keep it manageable. Whichever, do keep the weeds at bay with plastic sheeting or a cardboard mulch – having an out-of-control plot will not make you popular with your allotment neighbours.

2. Talking of your neighbours – they are a vital source of information. Ask them for advice, as they will know the soil and may have lots of ideas about what will grow easily.

3. Have a go with tomatoes and strawberries for a decent chance of success. Potatoes, rhubarb, beetroot and perpetual spinach are good for beginners, as they aren't too high-maintenance or thirsty.

4. Allocate some of your allotment to become a wildflower meadow to attract bees and butterflies.

5. Do involve the children – ask what they would like to grow and give them their own section to dig, weed and plant.

Special needs and **gardening**

Gardening can be life-changing for children with special needs. A Royal Horticultural Society study looked at children aged between 4 and 16 with diverse conditions including autism, Asperger's, Down's syndrome and dyspraxia. Regular time spent gardening led to improvements for all of them, particularly their cognitive and physical skills, as well as enhanced patience, concentration and social skills – some children formed friendships for the first time in their lives.[3]

Gardening is therapeutic. Working with soil can reduce tactile defensiveness and the unpredictability of the outdoors can also help to manage anxiety over routine and soothe the need to be in control. The delicate handling of plants is fabulous for improving fine motor skills. Gardening is a real example of learning and playing outdoors that is vital for all children, but it is those with special needs who have most to gain.[4]

Green [CHALLENGE] #19

Give up buying imported blooms and instead save carbon by growing your own. Try cosmos, cornflowers, delphinium and salvia for easy to grow, stunning flowers.

Wild garden **safety**

All gardens come with the usual elements of risk – for example, mowers and pesticides. A wild garden is often a safer place for little people and pets, but there are some poisonous plants worth avoiding for your peace of mind.

Top 5 plants to … avoid planting

1. Foxgloves
2. Rhododendrons
3. Lily of the valley
4. Yew
5. Poison ivy.

A great tit's guide **to life**

On a more philosophical note, when you are next gazing out into the garden, take a moment to consider that great tit, popping in and out of a nest box. What can we learn from our garden birds that would benefit our own lives?

Finding the perfect home

Many of us spend a lot of time fretting about getting on the property ladder, but we can learn a bit from the great tit. They are just glad to find a simple safe spot. Their requirements are a hole in a tree, a secluded hedge or four wooden walls.

People are often keen to upgrade, sometimes painfully overstretching themselves in the process. It's worth noting that 63 wrens were once found cohabiting in a nest box[5]: such tiny birds know the value of sharing body heat to stay alive. It goes to show that feeling crowded is simply a matter of perception and there are always benefits to be found from cosy living. Many children love sharing a room with a sibling, and a small home or flat certainly takes less time to clean.

It's not easy being a great tit parent you know

Babies fledge in the blink of an eye

The breeding cycle of garden birds shows that most young fledge in a matter of weeks. At two weeks many young birds are already spreading their wings and flying away. Baby swallows will set out for Africa soon after fledging.

It's not that rapid for us, but it does make you think about how quickly each phase is over and that we really should try and savour our children's childhood rather than feeling frustrated by the complications that our parental responsibilities add to our careers or social lives.

Forget possessions and get outside

As modern parents, we get distracted by all the material things we are meant to provide our children with, and all the educational clubs and opportunities we feel pressurized to offer them. In the end, all they really need is you, food, water, shelter, opportunities to socialize with other children and plenty of healthy exercise outdoors – just like young great tits.

It's not all meant to be fun

When I've had another broken night of sleep and there is crayon up the walls and someone is yelling at me to wipe their bum, I'm still thankful I'm not a great tit parent, battling the elements to find caterpillar after caterpillar for my demanding brood.

Childrearing, however you do it, whatever your other caring commitments and whatever your species, will push you to your limits and beyond.

Footnotes for Chapter 6

1 RSPB (2006). 'Birds and berries'.
  http://www.rspb.org.uk/discoverandenjoynature/discoverandlearn/funfactsandarticles/features/berries.aspx

2 Vaughan, A., (2013). 'Hedgehog population in dramatic decline'.
  www.theguardian.com/environment/2013/jan/29/hedgehog-population-dramatic-decline

3 Royal Horticultural Society (2010). 'Growing together: gardening with children and young people with special educational needs'.
  http://apps.rhs.org.uk/schoolgardening/uploads/documents/SEN_report2009-10_final_1049.pdf

4 Dr Rickinson, M. (2014). 'Growth through growing, students with special educational needs'.
  http://www.growingschools.org.uk/Resources/Downloads/Growth%20through%20growing%20(SEN).pdf

5 Holden, P. et al (2002). *The RSPB Guide to British Birds*. Pan Macmillan.

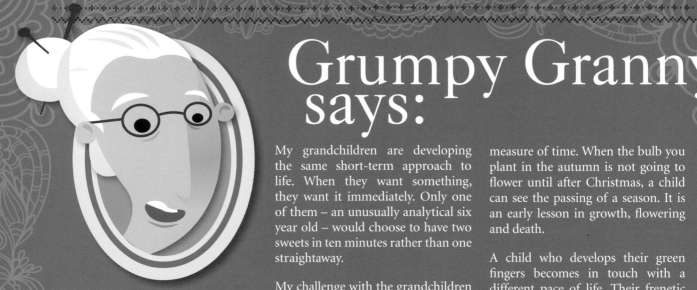

Grumpy Granny says:

Rush less, garden more

There is no excuse for parents who allow no time to just enjoy being. So many rush around, dragging their children from school to activities to parties to coaching. The kids gain new skills and have an exciting time while being encouraged to turn into buzzing, short-attention span kids.

The over-active parent syndrome even affects working mums. They pick up from school, then instead of going home to relax, they drag tired children to another time-consuming event that costs money.

The result, apart from exhausted parents, is children who cannot relax because they are used to being on the go. They fail to learn that good things can take time to happen. Delayed gratification is something they will never understand.

My grandchildren are developing the same short-term approach to life. When they want something, they want it immediately. Only one of them – an unusually analytical six year old – would choose to have two sweets in ten minutes rather than one straightaway.

My challenge with the grandchildren is to teach them that it is worth planning now for something that will not happen for weeks or months. I want to teach them slow living. The simplest way to do this is through the wonder of growing anything that the child has planted for themselves.

Lesson one: nothing happens straight away. Lesson two: still nothing – perhaps it is all a waste of time. Lesson three: a shoot, life, magic. They learn that it is best not to jump to rapid conclusions because sometimes a long wait is worthwhile.

It is an act of faith to plant seeds in soil and believe that they will grow. For a child brought up on an iPad, where every action creates an instant response, it is often impossible.

Learning delayed gratification does not need to be complicated: a hyacinth bulb held in place over a glass of water will grow roots, then leaves and finally a flower. This becomes a measure of time. When the bulb you plant in the autumn is not going to flower until after Christmas, a child can see the passing of a season. It is an early lesson in growth, flowering and death.

A child who develops their green fingers becomes in touch with a different pace of life. Their frenetic parents may even benefit from a slower nature-induced time scale as well – to the benefit of all the family.

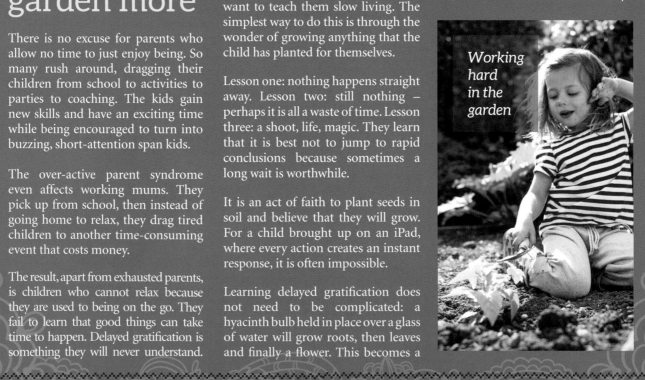

Working hard in the garden

How nature can nurture your family

Outside adventurers discovering nature

7

If our children were chickens, a trendy chef would have mounted a full-scale campaign by now. They would be knocking on the door of Number Ten, demanding basic rights and ethical welfare for our youngsters. 'Can you believe,' they would say, 'that these children are not free-range? In fact, they hardly get to go outside at all.'

The number of children being diagnosed with behavioural and emotional disorders showed a marked increase in the period 1999 to 2004.[1] Despite the lack of more recent official data, many professionals believe that mental health among young people has further deteriorated. They are particularly concerned because mental health services cannot meet current demands.[2]

Our children spend the vast majority of their time cooped up indoors, living their lives through television, games and the internet.[3] They don't exercise enough[4] and are growing fatter and slower than previous generations.[5] We wouldn't inflict such living conditions on a chicken. Why have we allowed this to happen?

Partly it is because we are so worried about their safety from strangers, traffic and injuries[6] that today's children rarely have the chance to be free, to simply be bored and mooch around outside. Many children that I met when I took primary schools around nature reserves were genuinely concerned that there might be crocodiles in the pond or wolves in the woods. Of course there are risks associated with playing outdoors, but if you keep your children inside too much, damage to them is guaranteed. This has been termed nature deficit disorder.[7]

Open the door to **nature heaven**

What does nature heaven look like? Is the whole family skipping merrily through flower meadows with a gentle breeze in their hair and a cute bunny frolicking nearby?

Oh no. Not a bit of it. Instead, there is mud – definitely mud. There are tears and snot running down chilly little faces. There are bumps and grazes to contend with. There are alfresco wees that soak trousers and shoes, and there are cold fingers and hopefully tired legs. The list of minor disasters can be endless.

So I won't promise that nature heaven is a picture postcard. Sometimes I walk my children back from the park in a torrential downpour with my three-year-old howling because she has rain down her back. I know that parents cosily peeking out of their windows will wonder if I can't afford a car.

Many of us feel immense pressure to have perfect time with our children when we get the chance. The soft-play park or the cinema are more guaranteed 'family fun' outings. The 'safer' options may be more predictable than a walk in the woods or a run around the park, but they will never truly compare. There is nothing like the moments of pure discovery that nature provides – when a snail pops out of its shell to look at you or a butterfly lands on your nose. There are calories burned, not for exercise, but just for the sheer joy of running down a hill. Most importantly, there are horizons, both literally and metaphorically, expanded in a world so, so much bigger than the ball pit or your lounge.

Hands-on exploration ...Mr Worm may not agree that children and nature go well together

In summary, kids who regularly play outdoors are fitter, calmer and happier than those who tend to stay indoors, and they are likely to sleep better too. Being active in areas of green space is also strongly linked with improving self-esteem and reducing negative feelings such as tension, anger or depression.[8] This applies to adults too, so the whole family will benefit. Resilience and stamina are developed. Children learn about risk without the convenient rules of a computer game. They learn the limitations and the strengths of their own bodies.

If you make a weekly space for nature in your lives, you will soon see the benefits in your own children.

Children need nature and nature needs children

Nature is pretty good at perfect pairings. Alongside the nettles we have soothing dock leaves, and when the apples ripen, the blackberries are ready for that delicious crumble. As the blue tit chicks hatch, the caterpillars emerge, providing perfect food for growing babies, and the hibernating bee wakes with the flowering of nectar plants.

Many species of wildlife, like the cheeky house sparrow, are declining in numbers

Here's another perfect pairing for you: nature and children. This growing generation need to care about their planet and do a better job than today's politicians, because nature is in serious trouble. Far more species are declining than increasing in the UK, including some previously common and much-loved species such as the house sparrow and the beautiful song thrush. The wildlife in our gardens and countryside is changing.

The incredible naturalist David Attenborough sums it up perfectly. 'The causes [of these declines] are varied, but most are ultimately due to the way we are using our land and seas and their natural resources, often with little regard for the wildlife with which we share them.'[9]

Climate change can inconvenience and cost us, but it is potentially catastrophic to plants and animals as they struggle to adapt to altered weather patterns.

What do you need to get in touch with nature?

You don't need to live in a national park or a rural idyll, you don't need a nature reserve or even a garden on your doorstep. So long as you can get to a small patch of green somewhere nearby, there is a whole world to discover with a million secrets to learn.

For our children's well-being and for nature's sake, it's time to re-wild the kids.

Owning a pet (or borrowing someone else's) is great for children

Top 5 ways to ... avoid nature deficit disorder

1. Balance screen time with outdoors time. For every hour the kids spend outside, they can have 60 minutes watching telly. If this is too big a change for you, then aim for just half an hour outside per day. We spend 4 minutes a day looking after our teeth, such a tiny part of us. Is 30 minutes really such a big commitment to care for the whole of our bodies and minds?

2. Walk, bike or scoot to school or nursery (if you live far away, you could still park 10 minutes from the school gate). It will boost your children's learning and help them blow off steam at the end of the day. Lobby your council for better pavements and traffic speed restrictions. High-visibility jackets may be necessary too.

3. Own a pet, or borrow someone else's. Animals teach children how to care for something other than themselves and to feel responsible for another's existence. The touch and stroking of a small furry body is proven to calm and relax both children and adults and it can even help with behavioural issues. If you are considering a pet, be aware that 99.9% of parents (OK, I made that statistic up) end up walking them or dealing with their faeces most of the time.

4. Put an app in it. Sometimes you have to work with the lure of technology. Here are a few ways to do so:

   - look for nature apps to help your children identify birds and mammals. Find apps that help you work out what bird is singing and check out the free Wild Time App from Project Wild Thing, which will give you brilliant activities for outside fun.

   - Stargazing is easier and more exciting with an app to accompany you. You'll be working out all the constellations in no time. Try Sky Map or Star Walk – these apps will name the stars in the direction you hold your phone or tablet.

   - Geocaching – searching for treasure using GPS on your smartphone – is green and active and your children will learn about geography, mapping and working together, all while exploring the great outdoors. Start with an easy-to-find cache (look at comments on a free geocaching app) rather than just the closest to you, which may be tricky to locate. Don't forget to take a trinket to swap if you want to take the treasure home. Key rings, foreign coins or little toys are good examples of items to leave.

   - Similar to geocaching, and fantastic in urban areas, is Munzee hunting. You use a free app on your smartphone to hunt and then scan QR codes, which score points.

   - Get online and track a bird. The British Trust for Ornithology has satellite-tagged cuckoos so you can choose your favourite and find out what he or she is up to, whether they are in the UK or the Congo or crossing the perilous Sahara Desert.

5. Lie on the grass with your child and look up at the sky. Ask them what they can feel, hear, touch, smell and see. Alongside bedtime cuddles, it's the purest time you will spend with them. Two minutes of your undivided attention can be worth hours of distracted contact.

Urban jungle

Our cities and towns are actually packed full of wildlife that is surprisingly tolerant of human activity. Look out for the urban fox as well as different types of deer, such as muntjac, and birds including the tropical parakeet, woodpecker and jackdaw.

In late autumn and winter, starlings will gather in massive groups, known as murmurations, to swoop and dance in shifting clouds across the sky, particularly in urban areas and at the coast. Birds of prey such as peregrine falcons love a high nesting point, and will often choose cathedrals or towers for raising a brood.

Head to an urban river for kingfishers and grey herons and dragonflies in the summer months.

Cemeteries are full of wildlife, such as this urban fox

How to inspire your children **about nature**

So you don't know your honey bee from your honeysuckle and you think the waggle dance is something that pop stars do? Don't worry, you don't have to be a naturalist. When I started out in environmental education many years ago I soon realized that I couldn't answer every question from children and this worried me. I was reassured by a more experienced colleague that one of the greatest techniques of outdoor educationalists is to answer 'I don't know, shall we find out?' to any question. I learnt alongside the children and my delight matched theirs. With nature, it is the discovery and the process of learning that is a major part of the fun.

Simply get outside and ask questions together. What is that creature doing? Is it asleep or dead? Can it fly? What might eat it? Your conclusions don't have to be right or wrong – just talking about wildlife is worthwhile.

Some species are worth the extra effort. To get you started, here are the top five UK species to make your child go WOW! Some will take more dedication, time and travelling than others but all will take your breath away.

You'll see they are rated on ease of finding (1 = trek all night, 5 = just outside) and wow factor (1 = that's interesting, 5 = mesmerising/awe-inspiring).

Green [CHALLENGE] #20

For this challenge, you will need to invest in a simple, cheap pedometer that clips on to your belt and counts your steps. Just one for the whole family will do, unless you get excessively competitive, in which case one each is needed. The challenge is simple – see who can do most steps in a day.

Every family member gets a chance to wear the pedometer for a full day and at the end of the day records the number of steps taken. A good amount to aim for is 10,000 and this will be more challenging for adults than children (as our strides are longer and lifestyles more sedentary). As a rough guide, my active three-year-old finds 11,000 easy in a normal day but their office-bound dad can often struggle to get above 4,000.

You'll soon clock on to the fact that going outside is essential to perform well in this challenge. It also makes children more helpful, as they are suddenly really keen to run upstairs to get their hairbrush.

'Hey sis, this is magnificent.'

'It's tiring being this cute', says little owl

The owl

Ease of finding = 4
Wow factor = 4

Whether it is as a cameo in The Gruffalo and Harry Potter books and films, or in a starring role in *The Owl Who Was Afraid of the Dark*, the owl is woven through the fabric of children's literature.

Of our native owls, the barn owl is the easiest to spot. Soft and silent, it is most often observed as a white ghost gliding through the dusk. Barn owls love to hunt in roadside verges, so driving along as the sun sets presents the perfect opportunity to see them.

For tawny owls, try woodland, or large gardens with old trees, parks and churchyards, particularly at night-time – spooky stuff. For a less scary option, the little owl can often be seen in the daylight perching on a tree branch or telegraph pole.

If you can find where an owl nests, you can collect owl pellets from beneath the nest for the ultimate lesson in food chains. Owls eat small rodents such as mice and shrews, which they swallow whole. The undigested bones and fur are then formed into brown pellets which the owl regurgitates, with the prey's fur cleverly arranged so that it is on the outside of the pellet and the sharp bones and skulls are carefully wrapped inside, thus avoiding a sore throat. Dissecting owl waste is undeniably a strange hobby, but it tells you a lot about the owl's diet.

The bee

Ease of finding = 5
Wow factor = 3

Did you know that half of British kids don't know the difference between wasps and bees? A National Trust study showed that of these same children, 9 out of 10 could recognize a Dalek.[10] This is scary in terms of their ecological knowledge, but it also means a child is more likely to get agitated when something buzzes nearby. Many a picnic was ruined this way.

Knowing the difference between mellow humble bumbles and the more aggressive wasps is a vital summertime skill. Mild-mannered bees will only sting if they are provoked or feel threatened. Here's a tip: bees are furry, and wasps are not. Bonus points to those who can spot a hoverfly too. They try to make themselves look hard as nails like a wasp, but are actually totally sting-free. Make sure your kids know their yellow and black code and they will know to stay away from wasps, delight in bees and impress their friends by acting cool around hoverflies.

A honey bee loading up on nectar and pollen in pollen baskets on its legs

Bees are vital to us as humans, not just for yummy honey but because of their role as pollinators. Think of them as mini-employees for society, busily working away for us while we sip juice (or Prosecco) on the patio. The bee is in real trouble though, with massive declines in the populations of most bee species. We currently have 24 species in the UK but within the past 70 years, two species have become nationally extinct.

The bumble bee

The avocet

Ease of finding = 2

Wow factor = 3

This bird represents the happy story of conservation. It was once extinct in the UK but recolonized at the RSPB's Minsmere nature reserve on the Suffolk coast. It is for this reason that the avocet is the RSPB's logo.

This bird is why we shouldn't ever give up – living proof that even a disaster can be overturned with hard work and dedication. The avocet is beautiful to look at, delicate in appearance yet gutsy in behaviour. Its distinctive black and white body perches on top of skinny wader legs, and a long up-turned beak looks impractical until you see it deftly delving in the sticky mud, seeking lunch. In springtime, its chicks are delightful little balls of fluff that are guaranteed to make you smile.

You can find the avocet on the east and south coasts of England. Head to an RSPB or Wildlife Trusts nature reserve where guides can point you in the right direction.

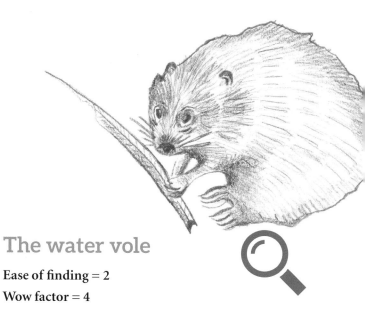

The water vole

Ease of finding = 2

Wow factor = 4

Ratty from Kenneth Grahame's *Wind in the Willows* was actually a water vole, not a rat. Personally, I think the water vole is far cuter and fluffier-looking.

You can find water voles munching the vegetation along river-banks and in marshes. They love to make tunnels beside the water both above and below the waterline.

This little mammal is having a tough time surviving since the escape of American mink into the UK's countryside. The mink loves nothing more than crunchy water vole for dinner and this is having a serious impact on water vole numbers. Habitat loss and summer droughts are big issues too. Recent research[11] shows that water voles have declined by a fifth in the UK since 2011.

If you want to see them, you need to find somewhere with a good network of ditches. They are still thriving in Snowdonia, the Fens and the Somerset Levels. Sit quietly and daydream while listening out for the characteristic 'plop' sound as they slip into the water.

Seeing a wild red deer is unforgettable

The red deer

Ease of finding = 3
Wow factor = 5

UK wildlife doesn't get more impressive than the majestic red deer. The largest of our deer species (males are about 135cm tall at the shoulder) are worth seeing all year round. For a truly pulse-raising, spine-tingling experience, you need to witness the rut in autumn, when stags compete with each other for access to the does. There is lots of bellowing, roaring and posturing, which can escalate into clashes of antlers and serious fights. This is definitely one for older children because it is intense and thought-provoking – you will have interesting questions about violence, death and sex to answer afterwards. Remind yourself that it's far better for your children to learn about these issues through nature with you than unsupervised on the internet.

You'll need to keep yourself safe by maintaining a distance and making sure the deer can't see you. It is worth going on organized safaris, which will get you as close as is possible without disturbing the deer.

Red deer are fairly well spread around the UK, and can be seen in the Scottish Highlands, Dumfriesshire, the Lake District, East Anglia and the south-west of England. For a real taste of the wild in an urban area, you can't beat the red deer in London's Richmond Park.

Go to the experts

A bat detector will turn a seemingly silent night into a buzzing, clicking world of activity, a moth trap will allow you to get close to creatures normally a distant flutter away, and a mist net will catch tiny birds so they can be examined, weighed and fitted with an identification ring by licensed scientists. Look out for local family-friendly sessions organized by the RSPB and Wildlife Trusts.

Party-trick wildlife

There is nothing like having a few party pieces up your sleeves to impress your children and for them to share with their friends. This is wildlife at its most fun.

A hidden froghopper

Nature can be really yucky, like this purple jellydisc fungus

Froghoppers

They look like yucky blobs of spit on a plant's leaves and stem, but if you gently probe the froth you will find a little creature. It is the larva of a sap-sucking insect known as the froghopper and the foam, known as cuckoo spit, protects them from predators. Look out for them on low plants, such as roses, dahlias, lavender and rosemary in early summer.

Dead nettles

The stinging nettle lies in wait for chubby little legs and unleashes a tear-jerking zing that feels like it will never go away. The dead nettle is its friendlier cousin. Learn to recognize it (by its white or purple flowers) and your children can impress their friends by being the only one who dares to pick up a nettle. Also, the nectar can be sucked from the base of the petals. You can find dead nettles all year round but they are easiest to spot when in flower in May and June.

Himalayan balsam

Little will make an unsuspecting child squeal with delight as much as the exploding pod of Himalayan balsam. When they are lightly touched they shower seeds all around. This isn't a native plant, and conservation bodies spend lots of time trying to eradicate it, so don't be surprised if it has been cut down next time you visit! August to October is the time of year for this activity and you can find the plant alongside riverbanks or ditches, in moist soil.

Nectar and no sting with the dead nettle

Leucistic birds

Ah, the joy of the complicated word and the pleasure your child gets, knowing they know something that no one else their age does. Leucistic (loo-kiss-tick) birds are those with white feathers instead of the normal plumage colour. It may be a blackbird with a funny white splodge on its wing or a jackdaw with a white head. The lovely thing about these birds is that you can soon recognize them as individuals. Luke is our personal blackbird that my family says hi to every time we spot him.

A blackbird with a difference: leucistic birds have white patches

Enjoy an explosion of seeds from the Himalayan balsam

Sticky willy

The fabulously annoying plant known as the cleaver or, more amusingly, sticky willy can liven up any stroll. It acts just like Velcro, so you can apply the long strands to the clothes of whoever is near you. The aim is to fix as many as possible to them before they notice.

Sticky willy

Disgusting nature

Older children particularly will enjoy a bit of yuckiness. What about the weird and wonderful forms of fungus, like the one on page 152 that looks disturbingly like a brain? This is the purple jellydisc fungus which forms a slimy, gelatinous mass of pinkish purple discs on the bark of fallen deciduous trees. They may also like to know that slugs have green blood and water scorpions breathe through their bottoms.

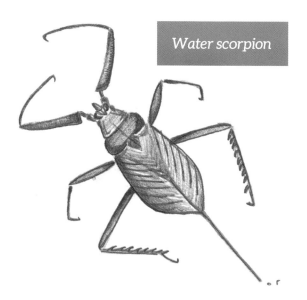

Water scorpion

Green #21
[CHALLENGE]

Have you ever been camping with your children? Many aspects of it are undeniably off-putting. These include unpredictable weather, the lack of personal space and the certainty of early mornings, but there is nothing quite like it for connecting your children to the outdoors. Make it your aim to spend at least one night a year under canvas with your family.

Children love getting involved in camping jobs, whether collecting firewood, knocking in tent pegs or filling up water containers. You'll soon see a whole new grown-up side to them.

Some campsites will permit fires, so have a look at the guide in Chapter 1 to find out how.

It's six in the morning – time for breakfast!

Wild campsite chorus

Being outside for much of the day and night on a camping trip means that you will have a brilliant opportunity to spot wildlife. Look out for shy deer and cheeky squirrels in woodland areas, and as dusk falls, watch out for bats.

Those early starts also mean that you will have the chance to enjoy and start to recognize birdsong, which will often start about an hour before dawn. The spring dawn chorus can be a bit overwhelming if you want to work out the individual voices, but it is handy to know that birds are quite ordered about it. The worm eaters such as the blackbird, robin and song thrush usually start first, as they can get looking for worms in low light due to their large eyes (this is where the saying 'the early bird catches the worm' comes from). Next we have the insect eaters, including the wrens and chiffchaffs. Finally, those with the smallest eyes wait for a little more light – these are the seed eaters, such as the chaffinch and house sparrow.

Later in summer is quieter, but you will still hear lots of birdsong. Listen out for owls at night too.

>> **Top 5 tips** for ...
successful camping

1. Have a practice night in your garden or a friend's garden if possible.
2. Check the weather forecast and bring appropriate clothes.
3. Freeze milk and any other suitable foods before you go so they stay cold and fresh in your cool box for longer.
4. Make sure heads face uphill: even a tiny slope will feel magnified when you are lying down.
5. Take a potty or bucket; it's much easier than taking kids to the loo in the middle of the night.

Is it Green or Gross...
to touch frogspawn?

Beach babies

The beach is one of the few natural paradises that most children get to explore on a yearly basis. Many commercial 'family' beaches are a strange mix of the untameable sea juxtaposed with all that humans like to keep them entertained: chip shops, ice-cream stands, fairgrounds and arcades.

Whether your favoured beach is a 'kiss-me-quick' spot next to the pier or a remote wilderness, there is plenty to do for children. All kinds of beach work whatever the weather, so don't just save the beach for sunny days.

For safe beach adventures, do remember to check tide times to make sure you aren't at risk of being cut off from land.

Dune jumping

Jumping or sliding down sand dunes offers a good opportunity to test the sport mode on your camera.

Crabbing

Crabbing is so much fun that I even did it on my hen weekend, with a hangover. With children, you need a decent child-to-adult ratio so you don't end up with live bait in the water.

To catch crabs, head to a harbour wall, or bridge over an inlet at high tide.

You will need:

- a pack of raw bacon
- a weight (a stone with a hole in or one that is knobbly enough to be tied to the bottom of the line is perfect)
- a fishing line or long piece of string
- a net
- a bucket filled with sea water

Simply tie the bacon and weight on to the end of your string and lower into the water. Wait patiently … then gently pull it up. Crabs will hang on to the bacon and can be caught in your net and carefully tipped into your bucket of sea water.

What can you find beside the sea?

Place your bucket in the shade and don't keep them out for too long – gently tip them back when you are done, or place them on estuary mud and see which one makes it into the water first; they know which direction to head in by instinct.

Under the pier

A stroll under the pier is well worth it. You'll find barnacles, mussels and seaweed growing on all available metalwork. Check for the squiggly casts of the lugworm.

She sells seashells

Collecting shells can keep children occupied for ages. The first step to becoming a proper conchologist (that's a scientist who studies shells) is to know what you've found. Some of the most commonly found are the long razor clams, the dark purple and pearly mussels, and the two connected little shells of the common clam.

A lovely craft activity is to buy a 3D découpage-style initial of your child's name and stick the shells on to it, or glue shells around an old photo frame.

Rock pooling

When the tide is low, it's time to hunt for creatures. You'll find rock pools on some beaches, but even if it is sandy you can still find life such as starfish and lugworms. Check the tide tables online or on an app (or a good old-fashioned booklet), then get in position an hour or so before low tide to maximize your time (and prepare your children with an ice-cream).

Older kids will enjoy snorkelling over the area as the tide comes in to see the difference water makes as anemones open up like flowers and small fish come out of hiding.

On a rocky beach

Rock pools are a magical microcosm of life under the sea. You might find starfish, crabs hiding under rocks, snails, small fish, barnacles and anemones. They are all real survivors – coping with the force of the waves, varying water levels and temperatures.

Look out for holes in the rocks made by boring molluscs or worms. Far from boring, these creatures are fascinating. The molluscs, known as piddocks, bore their way into rocks for protection. Worms make tunnels 2cm deep in the rocks so they can peep out to catch nutrients from the water. Look out for the chalky protective tubes that other marine worms create around themselves so that they become stuck on to rocks.

For rock pooling you will need:
- transparent buckets or clear tubs for viewing your creatures. Have more than one to keep predators and prey apart
- sturdy footwear with grips for slippery rocks
- sun cream and hats for summer
- no need for a net, use your fingers – they are much kinder. Approach crabs from the rear!
- a cheap disposable underwater camera for extra fun

Rocky beaches are interesting for their geology. Try scraping rocks with a coin or fingernail to see how soft or hard they are. The kind of rocks you find will help you work out which creatures may live there. Soft rocks are more likely to be home to boring creatures, but soft, sandy rocks can be hard to grip so are less likely to feature limpets or barnacles than hard rocks.

Some rocky beaches can be good for finding fossils. The Jurassic coast, stretching from Dorset to East Devon, is famed for its easily accessible fossils. Try Robin Hood's Bay in North Yorkshire, Hunstanton beach in Norfolk or Bracklesham Bay in West Sussex. Do keep children away from cliffs in case of landslides.

When you are fossil hunting, keep a look out for fool's gold (iron pyrite), a shiny yellow mineral found in sedimentary rocks such as limestone.

On a sandy beach

Look for bubbling air holes in the sand then dig, carefully. You may find a crab! Also, look for a squiggly sand pattern – you could find a lugworm below. It looks a bit like an earthworm with a segmented body, but can be thicker and longer.

Search for mermaid's purses – the leathery black egg cases of rays and sharks.

Is it Green or Gross...

that adult sea snails have a twisted body which means they poo on their own heads?

Freshwater fun

Looking for life under the water needn't be limited to the coast. Damming a stream will test your building skills and provide a perfect opportunity to meet some of the tiny creatures that live in fresh flowing water.

How to dam a stream

Find a small but flowing stream, ideally with a gravelly bottom so your boots don't get stuck, then collect stones, rocks, mud and sticks and do your best to block the flow. The water will build up on one side and you may find molluscs, flatworms and freshwater shrimps. An old ice-cream tub is perfect to collect some water and see what you can find.

Remember to break down your dam when you are finished.

Don't let the weather put you off

Building a temporary dam gives an opportunity to explore life in a stream

Baby, it's cold outside

Sometimes the lure of the television is too great to combat with a simple 'let's go outside'. That's when you need something a bit interesting, silly or competitive to persuade them that it is worth leaving the sofa's cosy grasp.

Green [CHALLENGE] #22

Find five different insects in your garden. A jam jar or old baby's bottle and a dry paintbrush will do for collecting them (use the paintbrush to gently sweep insects into the jar or bottle).

Top 10 ways to ... entice children out, whatever the weather

1. Make fat balls for birds out of lard, seeds and raisins (best done outside, as it is messy – see Chapter 6 for a recipe) and fill up the bird feeders.
2. Make a rain gauge (a jam jar marked with permanent marker will do) and guess the rainfall for the next hour or day. The winner gets chocolate.
3. Set squirrel challenges by putting peanuts in odd places, such as halfway up your slide.
4. Tame a robin: this takes patience and mealworms.
5. Take a flask of homemade soup or hot chocolate to the park with you.
6. Play with diluted food colouring in fresh snow to create snow art (or a murder scene).
7. Dare them to run naked to the end of the garden and back in the pouring rain. Warm pyjamas essential for afterwards.
8. Have a 'worm off' – the first child to find an earthworm gets to choose what's for dinner.
9. Bribery, pure and simple. You won't get a biscuit unless you play outside for 10 minutes. Those 10 will most likely become 30.
10. Make paper boats and find a puddle to float them in.

Sunflower

Safety and kit

Raising an active outdoors-friendly child is undeniably the best thing for their health, but scrapes and bumps come with the territory. Make sure you know what to do in the event of an accident, whether that's a child falling from a tree or an allergic reaction to an insect sting. Find a first-aid course aimed at parents near you.

It is always worth keeping a small first-aid kit in your bag. The contents will vary according to child and age, but plasters, antiseptic wipes, antiseptic hand gel and antihistamine cream are a good start.

Green [CHALLENGE] #23

Talk about your childhood to your children and tell them what you enjoyed doing. Was it rolling down sand dunes or building a dam in a stream?

Help them come up with a list of the top 20 outdoors things they would like to do in the next year. Ideally these should be free and fairly near to home. Write them up and decorate with pictures and display in your child's bedroom. Here are a few ideas:

- Grow sunflowers (plant them in springtime).
- Fly a kite on the beach (you could try making one).
- Go seal watching (you could see pups on your local beach in January. This is easier than you'd think because half the world's population of grey seals lives around the coast of the UK[12]).
- Stay up late on a cloud-free night to go stargazing (your garden or doorstep is fine but for best results, get as far away from artificial lights as you can).
- Wild swimming (have a look on www.wildswimming.co.uk for a map of safe places for outdoor swimming around the UK).

Wrap up warm and get moving

A charged mobile phone is an essential. Make sure your children know how to call the emergency services in case you are ever incapacitated.

There are a few other items that an outdoors family can't do without. These are pretty obvious: decent hats, thermal gloves, coats, sun cream, fleece-lined wellies (these don't cost much more and are worth it for keeping toes warm and avoiding welly rub). A waterproof suit or trousers are worth investing in and can be bought big so they last a couple of years. A sturdy back carrier with rucksack attachment is handy for carrying drink and snacks as well as tired little ones.

Is it Green or Gross...

to examine dead creatures? (protective gloves required!)

Nature-inspired names

Got a bump to name? Why not take inspiration from the natural world of flora and fauna? It doesn't have to be hippy-dippy unless you want it to be. No, these names are perfect for green prime ministers in the making. Go forth and save the world!

My top 10 ...
wild names

For girls
1. Willow
2. Fern
3. Flora
4. Poppy
5. Wren
6. Lily
7. Hazel
8. Daisy
9. Iris
10. Holly

For boys
1. Rowan
2. Robin
3. Ash
4. Jay
5. Basil
6. Heath
7. Berry
8. Sage
9. Oakley
10. Kes

Green [CHALLENGE] #24

A nestcam is the one sort of telly your kids should be watching. A nestcam linked to your TV or laptop will provide an insight into the normally secret care and hard work that goes into raising a brood.

They are easy to install and don't cost that much anymore. Be warned though, your children may become seriously attached to the babies and one or two usually won't make it, which is why most birds have big broods. Leave the nestcam in place when the chicks have fledged, as many birds will have a second go.

Footnotes for Chapter 7

1 Murphy, M. and Fonagy, P. (2012). Annual report of the Chief Medical Officer. 'Our children deserve better: prevention pays'. Chapter 10: 'Mental health problems in children and young people'. https://www.gov.uk/government/uploads/system/uploads/attachment_data/file/252660/33571_2901304_CMO_Chapter_10.pdf

2 Sedghi, A. (2015). 'What is the state of children's mental health today?' http://www.theguardian.com/society/christmas-charity-appeal-2014-blog/2015/jan/05/-sp-state-children-young-people-mental-health-today

3 Omega Pharma (2013). 'Over half a million school children spend no time outdoors'. http://www.omegapharma.co.uk/2014/03/over-half-a-million-school-children-spend-no-time-outdoors

4 Triggle, N. (2013). 'Children need more exercise – especially girls, study says'. http://www.bbc.co.uk/news/health-23778945

5 Lifestyles statistics team (2014). 'Statistics on obesity, physical activity and diet'. ibid.

6 Play England. (2012). 'Fear of strangers and traffic stop children playing outdoors'. http://www.playengland.org.uk/news/2012/08/fear-of-strangers-and-traffic-stop-children-playing-outdoors.aspx

7 Louv, R. (2010). *Last Child in the Woods: Saving Our Children from Nature-Deficit Disorder.* Atlantic Books.

8 Charles, C. and Loge, A. S., Children and Nature Network (2012). 'Health benefits to children from contact with the outdoors and nature'. http://www.childrenandnature.org/downloads/CNNHealthBenefits2012.pdf

9 RSPB (2013). 'State of nature'. http://www.rspb.org.uk/Images/stateofnature_tcm9-345839.pdf

10 National Trust (2013). 'Wildlife alien to indoor children'. http://www.nationaltrust.org.uk/article-1356398668159/

11 BBC (2013). 'Water voles "decline by a fifth"'. http://www.bbc.co.uk/news/science-environment-23981956

12 BBC (2015). 'Grey seal'. http://www.bbc.co.uk/nature/life/Gray_Seal

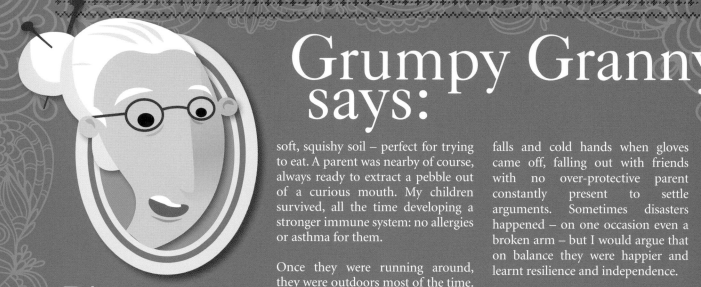

Grumpy Granny says:

Dirty up the kids

Two of my grandchildren are vacuum-packed and hermetically sealed. My son and daughter-in-law are bringing up their children with layers of 'protection' to keep them safe from the dangerous world outside their cocoon: even their friends are carefully selected. While it's great to see my grandkids covered in love, I think they are missing out on life.

My children and their friends were brought up as mucky outdoor kids. They spent time in the garden, even in winter. What a relief when the crying baby was being soothed by the priceless mobile of branches swaying in the breeze and the dappled sun flickering through the leaves. They progressed to crawling about on the grass: experimenting with stones, comparing their hard, cold surfaces to soft, squishy soil – perfect for trying to eat. A parent was nearby of course, always ready to extract a pebble out of a curious mouth. My children survived, all the time developing a stronger immune system: no allergies or asthma for them.

Once they were running around, they were outdoors most of the time. A fenced-in garden meant they could play almost unsupervised, with no rules. The garden suffered but the kids loved it. They built dens, climbed trees, squashed flowers, dug holes, fought with friends, peed behind a tree, and always, always used their imaginations and made their own fun.

OK, there were a few downsides. Muddy, dirty clothes and muck traipsed into the house. Tears from falls and cold hands when gloves came off, falling out with friends with no over-protective parent constantly present to settle arguments. Sometimes disasters happened – on one occasion even a broken arm – but I would argue that on balance they were happier and learnt resilience and independence.

So, I try and 'dirty up' the grandchildren when Mummy and Daddy are out of the way. Despite their sheltered upbringing, they respond. It takes them a bit of time to realize that it's OK and then they muck in, collecting sticks for a bonfire, getting smoke in their eyes, playing with hot embers and burning an inquisitive finger then forgetting the pain in the magic of discovering a woodlouse under a log.

In my day we used to live in mucky outdoor places

Green celebrations

There is so much more to celebrate than the set-piece events

8

What does celebration mean to you? All too often in a busy life we rush from one goal to the next, scarcely stopping to acknowledge how far we have come or how much we have achieved. Birthdays and Christmas can become less of a celebration and more of a logistical nightmare – getting the party sorted, having time to hit the internet before last-delivery dates, making sure Great-aunt Mildred has enough sherry.

It's easy to assume that celebrations are all about commercialization or just looking after other people's needs, but making time in our busy lives for celebration as a family is important. It's a break from the usual routine and a chance to appreciate our good fortune. The eve of our children's birthdays are one of the few moments many of us stop to acknowledge the day our lives changed for ever (or remember the 'joys' of labour).

Whatever you are celebrating, parties and family gatherings can be a recipe for environmental gloom. With chuck-away plastic plates, patio heaters, tat-filled party bags or unwanted gifts, it is tempting to put away your eco standards just for one day.

I'm not about to recommend high-maintenance alternatives that will crush the joy in your party spirit – deciding to crochet each party bag out of reclaimed wool is probably a recipe for insanity – but let's increase the times we get to celebrate, and do it in a manner that avoids waste and excess carbon usage. Your party will look thoughtfully planned without screaming 'green show-off'.

This chapter will help you navigate the moral minefields of having fun without the eco guilt.

What can we **celebrate?**

Instead of waiting for the predicable set-piece events to come along, why not make up your own special occasion or tradition? This will give you the freedom to do things your way, and to acknowledge the people or events you care deeply about.

My family tradition, a photo among the bluebells every springtime

For example, in my family, every May, come rain or shine, we head to a bluebell wood. It's lovely having photos of my children in a carpet of purple as they grow bigger every year and enjoying proof that spring is on the way. Sometimes we invite friends or family to join us and have a picnic lunch. Events in nature are great material for celebrations and you won't find commercialization of your own personal festival an issue. The great thing about alternative family traditions is that they often get passed on to the next generation.

Some traditional nature-inspired celebrations have largely been forgotten in modern life. Maypole dancing used to be a common sight across the UK. Could your community reinstate this celebration of the coming summer?

Top 5 ... natural events to celebrate

1. The return of the swallows. Make paper swallows to decorate the house, and look up migration route maps to learn about their journey. Swallows usually arrive back in the UK in April and May.

2. The first ladybird of the year. This depends on the weather, but they usually start appearing from mid-February onwards. Look carefully in undergrowth in your garden or park. How about a ladybird-shaped cake and a spotty dress code?

3. Harvest. Have you ever seen a real harvest in action? Your mission is to find a combine harvester at work without getting in the way, obviously. The harvest for wheat and barley is usually in August, but requires fine, dry weather.

4. Meteor showers. First, star-shaped sandwiches for dinner and some constellation-inspired art before heading outside to look up at the stars. Invite a couple of your children's friends for a sleep-over and make a real occasion of it. This can happen all year round – just check online for the next starry performance and the weather forecast for clear skies.

5. Organize an early-morning woodland walk for friends and family. You could do it on International Dawn Chorus Day (the first Sunday of May) and listen to nature waking up followed by breakfast together.

Wild birthday parties

Picture a typical four-year-old's birthday party. He's been awake since dawn, and didn't want any breakfast because it's all too exciting. Presents have been ripped open and he's dressed as a T rex (thanks, Auntie June). His entire preschool class has been invited to the local soft play centre and terrifying amounts of cake, crisps and sweeties have been consumed. The temperature on the top levels of the climbing area is that of a sauna. No one has puked in the ball pit … yet. A meltdown is inevitable and the parents are braced like a bunch of vulnerable herbivores.

It doesn't have to be this way. Embracing a more eco-minded party spirit will still have all the desired wow factor with less of the chaos.

Am I invited?

If you want your child to enjoy their birthday celebration, inviting one child for every year of their age is not a bad formula for youngsters. In the first years of primary school, when bonds are being formed, an inclusive whole-class party can work really well, but consider going joint with another parent to share the cost and effort. Older children may prefer an outing or activity with just a couple of friends rather than a full-on party.

Send recycled paper invitations or go paperless with e-invites to avoid school-gate stress from parents whose kids you haven't invited.

The party place

Don't feel you have to hire somewhere flashy in order to make the party a success. For spring and summer, an outside party can be wonderful, whether it's in your garden, at the local park, at the beach or nearby woodland. If your little one has a birthday in the colder months you can hire a local hall near a park cheaply with the reassurance of an inside space for food in case of rain. Most outdoor games can be brought inside (along with a floor picnic) – just check out these games ideas:

Game on!

Younger children often expect the usual faves, so enjoy musical statues, pass the parcel and pin the tail on the donkey, but it is also fun to have some more unusual options:

Build an amazing den

You will need:

Sticks, string, a tree, a tarpaulin sheet (if you are in the park with not many sticks) and some parents keen to muck in. If you are brave, you can test your handiwork by tipping water over the den while everyone sits inside. You could even have the party tea in the den.

See Chapter 1 for more den-construction tips.

Indoors option: kitchen chairs, a few bed sheets, blankets and torches.

Mini-beasting

You will need:

Some unmown grass, an old log pile or flower bed you don't mind being trampled on, insect boxes and paint brushes (to gently push the creatures into the pot) and an insect ID guide. You'll also need a prize for the child who finds the first woodlouse.

Indoors option: if you can't get outside, everyone can make their own insect out of homemade Play-Doh with some sticks and leaves for accessories. The prize goes to the freakiest creation. An insect hunt indoors with paper creatures will occupy them for 10 minutes.

For older children, a bush tucker trial is fun. Cooked spaghetti in green jelly or marzipan maggots, anyone?

Puzzle hunt

You will need:

Buy a cheap, age-appropriate jigsaw puzzle and draw a map in marker pen to show where the treasure is hidden on the back. Simply hide the bits of the puzzle indoors or out. The children have to find and make the puzzle to be able to locate the prize.

For older children you could have two puzzles with each team's pieces wrapped in different coloured paper. Split children into two teams and see who can get the treasure first. The map they follow could be more detailed and involve a larger area and the treasure could be buried.

Camping party

Put up a tent in the garden (older children could be challenged to put it up) and provide sleeping bags and marshmallows. A fun game is a sleeping-bag race, on tummies as worms or standing like a sack race. Eat the party food in the tent.

Yummy treats

A party is not a party without treats. Keep it locally sourced, organic where you can, and fairly healthy to avoid the sugar high and inevitable crash. These munchies are guaranteed to get the grown-ups nibbling too...

But how are you going to eat all this lovely food? Maybe you haven't got time to source local clay and make your own plates, but that doesn't mean you have to solve the problem with disposable plastic.

You could anticipate future parties and buy reusable plastic plates and cups that will be useful for BBQs and picnics too. You can find ones made from recycled plastic, such as old milk cartons.

If disposable is more practical for you, then go for paper or bamboo plates and cups, which will biodegrade. You can even get compostable cutlery.

Serve it all up on a plain paper table-cloth (or an old sheet) and put out colouring pens for them to doodle with.

Paper straws for drinking will add the final touch.

Stephanie's mum's easy cheesey party biscuits

Our illustrator, Stephanie, passed on this brilliant recipe from her mum. Rammed full of cheese and simple to make (ideal for children to help with), you will find the adults love these as much as the kids:

Makes 20 or so biscuits (depending on cutter size)

110g plain flour
Salt and pepper
170g grated cheddar cheese
60g soft butter
2 tbsp of milk

Preheat the oven to 180°C or gas mark 4 and grease a large baking tray.

Sift the flour and add a little salt and pepper. Add the cheese and butter and mix with a fork until crumbly. Add the milk gradually until it forms a firm ball (you may not need all the milk). Roll out on a floured surface and cut to shapes. Place on the greased tray and bake until slightly brown – this should take about 10 minutes.

Top 10 ... healthy, eco-minded party food ideas

1. Provide dough and toppings for the children to make their own pizzas.
2. Use wholemeal bread for sandwiches, or one side white and one brown.
3. Go super-healthy with falafels, pitta bread, veg crudités and dips.
4. Homemade bread sticks, cheese twists or easy cheesey party biscuits (recipe above).
5. Olives (stones out).
6. Chunks of Cheddar, halloumi (the squeaky cheese) and Edam.
7. Seasonal fruit to dip in organic, Fairtrade chocolate fondue.
8. Organic, Fairtrade chocolate buttons.
9. Homemade raisin and apricot flapjacks.
10. Fruit smoothies or homemade lemonade.

Decoration

Glitzy foil and bright plastic are the short cut to a party look. They call out to you from the shop shelf, offering you a good time. But you know you'll regret it the morning after, when you have to chuck them away into landfill.

Much better is a longer-term commitment that will stand the test of years. (Or simply admit it is a short-term thing, and opt for easily recycled paper options.)

Top 5 ...
eco-party decorations

1. Fabric bunting. You could even make your own no-sew version with pinking shears, ribbon and a stapler. Or you could use wallpaper samples for a super-frugal option.
2. Paper streamers.
3. Paper lanterns.
4. Paper honeycomb balls in bright colours.
5. A fabric banner, personalized with cut-out fabric or paper letters, glued on. Felt works well, as it won't fray.

Party bags

It is all about tat avoidance here. Plastic party-bag fillers that break in minutes (and aren't even that cheap) or masses of sweeties don't do the planet or the kids any favours.

Here's how you can provide fun party bags without the disposable factor:

Green #25
[CHALLENGE]

Go without helium balloons. Any balloon that ends up in the wider environment can kill wildlife and cause pollution – even the biodegradable latex ones take far too long to disappear. That doesn't mean sacrificing the party spirit, but instead sticking with good old air rather than helium (so no one will lose them into the ether) and disposing of them in the bin. If you really want to up the ante, source gorgeous Japanese paper balloons online.

Hey you! Did you know balloons are dangerous for marine wildlife like me?

Don't do party bags

I'm really not that mean! My children have left some of the loveliest parties they've been to with a slice of cake and a book or a small craft kit. One quality item can often be cheaper and more sustainable than lots of tat-tastic bits.

The It bag

On the arms of the coolest eco-kids this season you'll find the fabric or paper party bag. You can even make your own out of magazine pages or newspaper if origami doesn't terrify you.

No such thing as a free meal

Put those kiddies to work to make their own party-bag fillers. Try an activity where they decorate biscuits, paint a brooch or plant a seed in a little terracotta pot that they have painted or adorned with stickers.

Avoid packaging overload

Try to buy in bulk instead of items that are individually packaged. Cars, pens, wooden jewellery, marbles and hair accessories are all good bulk-buy options.

Fill me thriftily

You need not spend a fortune. Print out a few colouring pictures of whatever the kids are into at the moment, or make (or just print out) word searches and puzzles. A word search with the names of everyone who went to the party is a nice touch – online generators make this as easy as ABC. Double-check that no naughty words have accidentally been created though!

If you are feeling creative, homemade chocolate truffles are lovely fillers, or take all those broken crayons and melt them down and reset in star-shaped moulds (melt similar colours together, otherwise you'll end up with murky brown).

More eco-fillers

Here are a few more party-bag filler ideas for a range of budgets and ages:

- packs of wildflower seeds
- Fairtrade chocolate
- recycled bookmarks
- wooden yo-yos
- wooden dice
- wooden cup-and-ball games
- gemstones
- small colouring books
- rubber and wood stamps with ink pad
- outdoor chalks
- RSPB wildlife and nature pin badges
- animal masks made from card (recycled or sustainably sourced).

Putting the green into your traditional **celebrations**

If you mark every occasion as the party industry would like, then across the year you will be spending a fortune as well as regularly overlooking your eco-intentions. A few little tweaks can really make a difference to how green your family celebrations can be.

Naming days and christenings

Planting a tree for the birth of a child, or as part of their naming day or christening, is a lovely way of linking them to the natural world. Make sure you choose a native tree, such as a rowan, silver birch, fruit tree or if space is an issue, a small bay or rose in a pot.

The rowan is the Celtic tree of life and is traditionally planted to celebrate the birth of a new baby. Most native trees are associated with particular myths and folklore.

Plant a tree for your new baby

The symbolism of trees

- Rowan for a new baby
- Oak for strength
- Wild pear for loyalty
- Birch for renewal
- Crab apple for love
- Willow for imagination
- Hazel for creativity
- Ash for wisdom
- Apple for youth and health
- Cherry for love and affection
- Cedar for protection
- Elder for new life

It may be best to avoid hawthorn though, as apparently it results in contradiction!

Oak leaves and acorns

Nature doesn't always play nicely. You could plant two trees to have a back-up in case one dies. By the time the child is old enough to know about it, the tree will most likely be well established. Consider your options if you intend to move house, as any move will stress the tree or shrub (nearly as much as it will you!). Younger specimens less than five years old are more likely to survive. Ideally you would move deciduous plants when they are dormant during the winter, and evergreens at the end of winter, just when the soil is starting to warm up.

Wet the soil well the day before moving and get excavating to work out how widely the roots spread. Dig round the roots, keeping as many intact as possible. Loosely tie the branches to keep them protected before lifting, and wrap the roots in damp sacking. Replant as soon as possible into a hole bigger than the one you took it from. Pack the soil down and keep well watered in dry weather. (If all this sounds a bit much, instead you could make a donation – for example – to save rainforest in South America or to protect orang-utan habitat in Borneo.)

Fresh air on New Year's Day starts the year the right way

Is it Green or Gross...

to save your placenta in the freezer and then plant it under the naming-day tree? It will provide nutrients to the growing plant but may disturb your relatives (although less so than offering round a placenta smoothie).

New Year's Day

Start the year as you mean to go on by ignoring the sales and getting some fresh air with all the family, however hungover you feel. Grey seals have their (incredibly cute and fluffy) babies in December and January, so find out if there are any at your nearest beach.

You will also need some resolutions for the year ahead. Make these less about what you won't do and more about what you will. This is about action, not deprivation. Could you vow to get outside with the family every day, eat only seasonal veg or cycle to work twice a week? These positive targets will help you all feel fitter and healthier.

Valentine's Day

Forget overpriced chocolates and imported flowers and most certainly forget an overcrowded restaurant. Instead, take a leaf out of nature's book for a memorably romantic day.

According to legend, every year on Valentine's Day Mother Nature calls all the birds together to choose their mates. As usual, myths have a grain of truth at their heart, and it is around now that avian flirting and posturing really gets going.

The lengthening days signal that it is time to get frisky. This leads to perfectly timed babies, whose arrival coincides with milder spring days and an increased food supply.

This V Day, take the focus off that sickly-sweet pink version of romance by putting up a nest box ready for those baby birds. That's not to say that you shouldn't cook a posh dinner and make a card for your love too, but avoid the commercialization of this day which has its roots in nature.

Passover

Passover is also known as the festival of springtime because it coincides with the start of the grain harvest in Israel as well as the lambing season.

Celebrate with homemade, ethically and locally sourced Passover feasts and think about the natural connection between the Jewish tradition and eco consciousness. After the Seders are complete, make sure you share out leftovers to reduce waste.

Why not grow your own karpas (leafy green vegetables)? For growing parsley, you will need to get started at least two months before Passover (many people involve the children in the planting as an activity to celebrate Tu B'Shevat). Sow the seeds in a pot of soil and keep moist on a warm, bright windowsill as there is still the risk of frost outside. For a less traditional, but much quicker option, use quinoa. Quinoa is kosher and grows into yummy crunchy sprouts in just a couple of days.

Easter

You are going to need chocolate and lots of it, so make it Fairtrade, organic and lightly packaged.

Easter's theme of new life is a good excuse for time outside. Look for lambs on your family strolls (although don't touch sheep if you are pregnant) and cute bunnies too, although there is some debate as to whether the Easter bunny is actually the larger hare – the pagan symbol of love, growth and fertility.

Green [CHALLENGE] #26

Grow your own karpas

Soak half a cupful of quinoa in water for a couple of hours, rinse and drain off as much liquid as possible. Place into a container and cover loosely with a damp piece of cloth or kitchen roll. Keep in a cool place, out of direct sunlight. You will now need to rinse and drain a couple of times a day until the sprouts are a couple of centimetres long. Store them in the fridge until you are ready to munch. They will keep for a week or so.

Some people believe the hare was the first Easter bunny

Eggs and chicks are symbols of new life

Earth Day

Every year, events are held worldwide to demonstrate support for environmental protection. Find out this year's Earth Day theme and whether there are any activities local to you, or come up with your own ideas as to how you can mark it. Maybe it will be a technology-free day, or having a no-electricity hour.

Green #27 [CHALLENGE]

Using foods to dye eggs is an educational and eco-friendly Easter activity.

First, choose the colour you'd like your eggs, and gather the required ingredients:

Pink – raspberries or beetroot (100g)

Yellow – ground turmeric (1 tbsp)

Orange – carrots (100g) or paprika (1 tbsp)

Green – spinach (200g)

Blue – blueberries (150g)

Vinegar

4 uncooked free-range eggs – whiter ones will become a purer shade of the dye.

Bring a small pan of water to the boil (approximately 500ml) and add your dye (cut up if it is carrots or beetroot). Next, add a tablespoon of vinegar and your uncooked eggs.

Simply boil for 10 minutes and remove from the heat. Leave the eggs in the water for about an hour until cool. For a deeper colour, refrigerate the eggs in the dye overnight.

Ramadan

Ramadan has its roots in a pagan festival, where the fasting was from moonrise to moonset. Nowadays, abstaining from food and drink happens from sunrise to sunset, and it is a chance to think about becoming more frugal and to consider how your food choices impact the environment. This makes the month of Ramadan a brilliant time to make a shift to becoming a greener family.

Make sure you don't overcompensate by having lavish meals when you do eat; focus on seasonal, local and sustainable produce and your month may just change your habits for the rest of the year.

What other environmentally bad habits could you give up for the month?

Midsummer's Eve

This originally pagan festival to mark the summer solstice is a lovely opportunity to let the children stay up late and be outside. Light a fire (see Chapter 1 for how to do this safely), make flower and oak leaf garlands to wear in your hair, and see if you can recreate Stonehenge out of chunks of chocolate sponge cake. Then eat it.

Diwali

Diwali, the festival of lights, is traditionally about new beginnings and the triumph of good over evil and light over darkness. To keep yours eco-friendly, get back to the roots of this celebration with homemade sweets, and clay diyas (oil lamps) or natural candles rather

Halloween wildlife in all its beauty

than electric illuminations. Avoid setting off lots of fireworks and instead focus on simple eco-friendly activities, such as making beautiful rangoli artwork on the floor, using coloured rice. If you'd like to make your own beeswax candles, see how later in this chapter.

Halloween

Why buy a plastic pumpkin when you can have a real one? See if you can use every bit of your pumpkin. You can dry the seeds and thread them with a needle on to cotton to make a necklace, or roast them in a little oil for a tasty snack. You can make soup or curry from the

Top 5 ... eco-friendly costume ideas

1. Accessorize a witch costume with a cauldron made from a papier-mâchéd balloon. Cut off the top section to make a cauldron shape, then glue an egg carton to the base (four egg sections). Finally, paint it all black and add a string or ribbon handle.
2. Snap to it as a crocodile. Find a green outfit for your child and affix one leg of green or brown tights stuffed with newspaper to their bottom for the tail. For the crocodile's head, you need a rectangular cardboard box the size of a large shoebox or bigger, and preferably longer. Make a head hole at one end and a big gaping mouth at the other end. Cut nice sharp teeth out of white card to stick around the croc's mouth. Add some blood on the teeth for added fear factor. Paint the head green, not forgetting scary yellow eyes (scrunched-up tissue paper works well).
3. A Lego brick is a fun costume idea. You need a large rectangular cardboard box to fit around the child's torso and six paper bowls. Paint the box and the bowls with gloss or water-based paints. Glue or tape the bowls to the box in Lego formation. Make a head hole and two arm holes and remove the

bottom part of the box. Wear clothes and face paint the same colour for maximum effect.
4. Scary Mummy is coming to get you! Cut an old bedsheet into bandage-width strips. Wrap the strips around legs, torso and arms, using safety pins to keep them in place and pin to their clothes so it feels secure. Face paint can add the necessary white face and ghoulish eyes. Add more bandages, covering the hair. The child should wear a close-fitting top and tights or leggings in a pale colour.
5. The super-sized pumpkin works for any age. Take an over-large orange top and using a black marker pen draw a pumpkin face on it and lines up and down (roughly four on each side). With the child wearing the top, stuff it with pillows and anything soft, such as spare clothes, until it is as round as possible. You'll need to tie a cord or ribbon around the waist to keep it secure. Accessorize with green tights and an orange face.

flesh. The flesh will freeze well if you don't have time to deal with it or want to save it for a Thanksgiving pumpkin pie. Make sure you buy your pumpkins just before the day so they haven't gone off.

Make ghoulish cupcakes with the kids to give out to trick-or-treaters. If you want to go beyond the homemade sheet-over-the-head ghost outfit, source a secondhand costume or see the ideas on this page. And when you set out trick-or-treating, it is all about the wind-up torch for eco light (and toned arms). You could even make your own felt buckets.

For an exciting activity, a scavenger hunt in the dark with just those wind-up torches is fun. Keep it natural, seeking a pebble, two types of leaf, or hide some glow-in-the-dark objects in the undergrowth.

Younger children will enjoy making wands out of sticks decorated with ribbons or colourful pipe cleaners. In

*Look out for
tawny owls on
a dusk walk*

folklore, apple wood is magical and is a favourite with witches. Harry Potter's wand was made from holly (traditionally to provide protection against evil spirits) and Hagrid's from oak, the tree of strength.

Remind your kids that many of the creatures associated with Halloween aren't that spooky. You could teach them more about owls, spiders and bats, and go on a dusk walk to see if you can see or hear any.

Bonfire night

Fireworks and bonfires increase the amount of particulate pollution in the air and disturb pets and wildlife. This means that it is more eco-friendly to go to an organized event, but if you are planning your own firework party, here is how to limit the damage:

- Check your bonfire carefully for wildlife before igniting. If you are lucky enough to find any hedgehogs, frogs or toads, pick them up wearing gloves and relocate to a pile of leaves or under a shrub or hedge.
- For fire-making tips, see Chapter 1.
- Aim your fireworks away from trees, hedgerows or nest boxes. This will minimize the disturbance to all those birds and creatures wondering what on earth is going on.
- Make sure you tidy up afterwards, as dead fireworks or cans can trap small creatures.

Green [CHALLENGE] #28

See how high you can get a ripe cranberry to bounce.

Thanksgiving

The origins of Thanksgiving are decidedly natural – to celebrate and give thanks for the safe bringing in of the harvest. Source your food locally, make that pumpkin pie at home and buy a free-range turkey, or prepare a vegetarian feast instead. Using leftovers after a big feast is important too. Turkey curry, turkey sandwiches, turkey risotto, turkey soup ... you get the idea!

The winter solstice

The shortest day of the year is a time to reflect, draw your loved ones near and seek light in the darkness. You could decorate the house with paper snowflakes and make candles out of rolls of natural beeswax, a lovely alternative to traditional paraffin candles with a honey-sweet scent.

All ages will enjoy making candles, since there is no melting required. Just help younger children with cutting.

Makes 4 beeswax candles, or cut the sheets up to make more.

You will need:
- 4 beeswax sheets (they usually come in squares of 20cm by 20cm (8" x 8")
- 1m (40") of wick (this will often be available as a package with beeswax sheets)
- Scissors

Working in a warm environment, firstly cut your wicks so that they are about 5cm longer than each sheet of wax. Lay a wick on the edge of a sheet with the spare poking out from each end. Now start rolling the wax around the wick. You'll need to be firm at first to make sure there are no gaps. Then, roll gently, keeping it as straight as you can (but the candle will still work if a bit wonky, so do let the kids have a go). Don't press too hard.

When you reach the end of the sheet, fix it in place by smoothing the join gently with your finger. Choose which end will be the top of your candle and trim the wick to approximately 1.5cm long. Cut the wick away from the bottom of the candle.

Your candle needs a heatproof dish or a candle holder and it is ready to burn.

The Christmas robin

Christmas

Overall, Christmas isn't good for the environment. Factor in extra travel, unnecessary consumption, permanently switched-on twinkly lights, miles of gift wrap and petrochemical-based fake trees and things certainly aren't looking green. But Christmas helps us survive the dark days of winter, so let's not cancel the fun just yet.

On the positive side, many polluting industries stop work over the festive season, which gives the environment a brief chance to recover. And, with a little thought, it is possible to have a more sustainable break without sacrificing any of the frivolous enjoyment.

Firstly, choose a real tree, with the roots still on so it can be replanted in your garden. To make life easier, you can replant it still in the pot, but do make sure you increase the size of the pot as the tree grows. Even if it only survives a few years of service (coming into the warm then back out to the chill is stressful), you will still have saved money and waste.

If your garden is big enough, you could invest in two trees with roots on and alternate which one has to suffer the balmy temperatures of indoors while the other gets a turn out in the cold (maybe with fairy lights on).

If you can't afford a roots-on tree, or don't have space for replanting, make sure you mulch or compost the rootless one after Christmas – your local authority can help. You could choose an all-wooden tree that will be reused every year. They are sculptural and surprisingly affordable.

To decorate your house, bring the outside indoors.

Holly and berries

Evergreen leaves, holly berries, mistletoe and pine cones will all look wonderful and you can make your own wreath for the front door.

Don't forget the Christmas robin. Top up your bird feeders and test the children to see if they know how far his red breast extends – is it just his tummy or right up to his eyes?

Is it Green or Gross...

to give someone the rather squidgy chocolate truffles lovingly made by the children?

Is that for me?

Support your butcher and buy a free-range turkey reared locally, and source your seasonal veg locally too.

Eco gifts

Whether it is for Christmas or birthday, mass gift-buying is one of the pleasures and pains of being a parent.

When it comes to selecting presents, the first rule is to avoid spending money where possible. Can you give your time instead? Many tired parents would love a day of babysitting their kids, or how about gardening for Granny, decorating for your sister or baking your best friend a cake of their choice? Homemade gifts are always a big hit, such as jam, chocolate truffles or sloe gin.

Of course you will have to open your wallet, but try to

support your high street, avoiding retailers who keep their doors pinned wide open in freezing weather, wasting precious energy.

Garden and wildlife gifts are brilliant for the environment. A nectar-rich plant is a gift for bees and butterflies, and a Christmas box bush is a lovely choice. It provides a source of winter nectar for early bees, is easy to grow and gives a glorious scent in the coldest months. Bird boxes, bulbs and bird feeders (for example, a nyjer seed feeder to attract goldfinches) can bring a lot of pleasure through the year too.

For children, try nature magazines, some binoculars or a wormery. Membership to organisations such as the RSPB or Wildlife Trusts can open up new horizons. Where possible, choose sustainable wooden toys: they are far lower in carbon and more likely to be passed on to the next generation. You can also buy battery-free torches and wooden phones, wooden construction kits and Fairtrade soft toys. Older children are inordinately delighted with a paper present – that's the good old-fashioned ten-pound note. It may feel lazy to you, but having their own money means a lot, and you can be sure they will buy something they really want.

Don't be shy – ask people what they want and drop a few hints yourself. Nothing is worse for the environment than something that ends up straight in landfill, however gorgeous it may seem to the giver. And as for the guilt of re-gifting or eBay-ing unwanted items? Get over it: it's the greenest option for rejected gifts.

Greetings **cards**

If you love to send cards, seek those made from sustainable forests that support a nature charity. You could buy blank cards and make your own, or get the children to help cut up and stick old Christmas cards on to coloured card at Christmas. Don't forget to save this year's cards for cutting up next year. They're great for DIY gift tags too.

If you'd rather save the carbon, consider donating the equivalent to charity and phoning the people you care about.

Wrap attack

Try wrapping up gifts in old magazines. Wildlife ones are great, as are the glamorous ones such as Vogue for the ladies. These can be easily recycled, as can brown paper. Your children's pictures will also make very cute, customized wrapping paper, as will fabric remnants from craft projects. And in this day and age of the sat nav, dig out those neglected old maps and use them too. A few re-used ribbons will finish off the package, as well as a sprig of holly or mistletoe for Christmas gifts.

Capture the **moment**

So much of life is about rushing busily from one thing to the next, so one of the joys of celebrations is a chance to pause and take stock. It's lovely to record your special events and milestones, but the smartphone culture can mean that we end up with loads of mediocre snaps, rather than beautiful prints to frame.

Don't make the mistake of letting the digital world be your only record. A scrapbook for each child, where you write down their funny sayings and stick a lock of hair from their first haircut, is valuable too.

Urban
jungle

A street party is the ultimate eco celebration in urban (and suburban) areas. It's a brilliant way of getting to know your neighbours. Look into closing the street to traffic with your council or highways agency. It is fabulous for children to be able to reclaim the street, so organize lots of active games and scooting on the road.

Phil Barnes's top 5 tips
for... taking brilliant photos of children outside

Here are some top tips from this book's very clever photographer:

1. Take your children on an adventure somewhere new, where their imaginations can run away with them. That spirit will be reflected in the photographs you take.

2. Don't just try and pose your children, take action shots during games like hide and seek, or give them piggy-back rides to get them smiling.

3. Younger children are usually better to photograph in the morning when they're full of energy. You could take older ones out later in the day to find some lovely late afternoon to early evening light, particularly during the summer months.

4. Think about their clothing – patterns can look too busy against a natural setting, and shades of green and brown can merge into the background.

5. Make sure your shutter speed is at least $\frac{1}{250}$th of a second or on a sporty mode to catch some of the faster action and fleeting expressions.

Grumpy Granny says:

There's more to birthdays than presents

Celebrate for the sake of our future

Why celebrate? It's a waste of precious resources. Things are bought that no one really wants. Little kids learn to rip open one present then immediately look for the next. They have no time to consider, enjoy and appreciate, as they are overwhelmed by the conveyor belt of stuff.

When it comes to birthday parties, even sane parents can behave out of character. They book parties at venues they cannot afford, buy fancy birthday cakes to impress other parents, fill party bags with bits and pieces that will soon be chucked away. They invite so many children the cost is multiplied to ridiculous levels.

For once, Grumpy Granny will not complain. To celebrate any stage of life, from birth to death, is essential, and ultimately there is no right or wrong way. Children should know that events such as the anniversary of their birth is special, that wedding anniversaries matter, and that remembering when their hamster died is important. They are all part of our journey through life. Events make our lives feel significant and they should be marked.

For me, celebrating birthdays with my seven grandchildren is a reminder of what matters most in life. Their anniversaries are a reminder of the importance of our environment, of why it matters to care. Being green is not just a fad, it is what life is all about.

We must look after this planet to the best of our abilities for the future of our children and our grandchildren. We must not act in the short term but behave in a way that is good for the future. That is why I encourage my grandchildren to preserve resources, protect biodiversity, reduce pollution and cut their emissions. I want my grandchildren to see their grandchildren born into a world that is still healthy and strong.

Acknowledgments

This book wouldn't have been possible without Phil Barnes's beautiful photography, the incredible support of my grandparents Maurice and Muriel Brook, Marie (my mum) and Clive Francis, Stephanie Laurence's illustrations and gardening advice, my husband Chris's wonderful love and support and of course my own greenish babies.

Many thanks to my dad, Chris Skinner, for imparting years of wildlife knowledge, despite me not listening in my teenage years. I'm also very appreciative to both High Ash Farm (www.highashfarm.com) and Caroline Blincoe for providing beautiful backdrops for the photos.

Thank you to my editor, Sadie Mayne, for culling both my waffle and my overused exclamation marks!! And Tara Greaves for reading an early version.

So many other people have been involved in this book, giving inspiration, ideas, recipes, expertise, time and support and for giving me opportunities over the years. In no particular order...

Tatterfly Wild Gardens (www.tatterfly.co.uk)

Dan, Wilbur and Wren Skinner

Rowan and Liz Skinner

Helen Woods

Helen Deavin

Rebecca and Stephanie from Really Eco Baby

Grumpy Granny

Steve Rowland

Erica Auger

Aggie Rothon

Caroline Baines

Laura and Adam McCaw

Vic Purling

Jo Stevenson

Alex Lowe

Bambino Mio

Jemma Moran

Toby Hammond

Dan Green

Mark and Heidi Evans

And of course, the wonderful team at Green Books, particularly Niall Mansfield, Megan Entecott and Lindsey Tate.

Resources

Inspiration

Credible and thought-provoking, the following magazines, websites and books will give you insights into eco-family life and, with their online forums, provide the support of a green parent community.

The Green Parent magazine – a beautiful magazine with a useful website and forum. www.thegreenparent.co.uk (UK).

Green Child – a magazine aimed at Canada and America but relevant for all. Reads well on a tablet. www.greenchildmagazine.com (US and Canada).

The Natural Parent magazine – this magazine offers lots of lovely articles with particular emphasis on gentle parenting. www.thenaturalparent.com.au (Australia).

A Mighty Girl – a brilliant website recommending the best books, toys and movies for 'smart, confident and courageous girls'. The blog is essential reading for all those with daughters. Offers location-specific info. www.amightygirl.com (UK, US and Canada).

Green Baby Guide – this website is by two mothers raising green babies in Eugene and Portland, Oregon. Lots of interesting articles, recipes and suggestions. Great product reviews too. www.greenbabyguide.com (US).

Happier People Healthier Planet: How Putting Wellbeing First Would Help Sustain Life on Earth by Teresa Belton (Silverwood, 2014). A wonderful book encouraging you to rethink your lifestyle and work out what it truly means to be happy. When I get that 'I want to buy something' urge, Teresa's book reminds me that I don't have to purchase things I don't truly need.

Project Wild Thing started as a film-led movement to get more children outside (do watch the film). It has now become a growing movement of organisations and individuals who care deeply about the need for free-range, roaming kids in the twenty-first century. The website is a good source of ideas and a way of connecting with like-minded people and organisations. www.projectwildthing.com (UK).

Red Sky at Night: The Book of Lost Country Wisdom by Jane Struthers (Ebury Press, 2009). This truly wonderful book is full of all the old country folk law that is being forgotten, such as the names for gatherings of animals (how lovely is 'a charm of goldfinches'?) and how you can predict the weather by looking at the sky.

Information

There is plenty of information on the web, but how do you know what you can trust? Here is a good starting point for useful and practical advice, whether you are struggling to breastfeed, want to nourish your children with healthy, seasonal food or go further with your wildlife gardening.

Baby-led weaning – if you are interested in the messy but wonderful adventure that is baby-led weaning, this website should be your first port of call. You'll find out about the science, the practicalities and gain recipe ideas. If you are from America, Canada or Australia, the 'hands-across-the-ocean' thread on the forum makes it all the more relevant to you. www.babyledweaning.com (UK).

La Leche League offers invaluable **breast-feeding support**, from lots of information to brilliant volunteers on the phone who can help you through the hard bits. www.lalecheleague.org (UK).

Find out about **Forest Schools Education** at www.forestschools.com (UK).

Go further with your wildlife gardening with this beautiful book, *The Wildlife Gardener: Creating a Haven for Birds, Bees and Butterflies* by Kate Bradbury (Kyle Books, 2013).

The wonderful Nikki Duffy wrote this book's lovely foreword. She also authored *The River Cottage Baby and Toddler Cookbook* (Bloomsbury Publishing, 2011) which will help you feed your little one in a healthy, sustainable way. Great for the whole family.

Richard Mabey's *Food for Free* is the perfect foraging companion; opt for the Collins Gem guide (2012) if you want to take it out and about, or the beautiful (but more expensive) coffee-table version (HarperCollins, 2012).

Wildlife and conservation organisations

Whether you seek a worthwhile cause to support, or are interested in learning more about nature and conservation from charities, many of whom offer wonderful resources for children, here are some of the best.

- In the UK we are spoilt for choice for conservation charities offering lots for families:

The RSPB taught me (nearly) everything I know. The nature reserve network is brilliant for first-hand experience of wildlife and families are welcomed. The youth membership, called the Wildlife Explorers, is great for children and they will love the magazines arriving in the post just for them. www.rspb.org.uk (UK).

Not just about stuffy old buildings, **The National Trust** is leading the way in encouraging children to get hands-on with nature, offering activities, ideas and family facilities at many sites. www.nationaltrust.org.uk (UK).

There is a **Wildlife Trust** near you, caring for your local wildlife and wild places. Each year, they connect 300,000 children with nature through education programmes and Forest Schools and protect wild places where children can spend long days of discovery. You'll go home with leaves in your hair, mud on your hands and a little bit of nature in your heart. Find out more about their junior membership branch, called Wildlife Watch, and family events at www.wildlifewatch.org.uk (UK).

The Woodland Trust works to protect woods because they are 'truly magical playgrounds where children can have exciting adventures'. I quite agree! The children's membership is worthwhile and they will be sent weekly outdoors challenges by email. www.woodlandtrust.org.uk (UK).

- Global environmental charities:

Tackling big issues such as climate change, biodiversity loss and pollution can really benefit from a global approach.

Friends of the Earth International addresses topics such as climate justice and energy, forests and biodiversity. www.foei.org.

The World Wildlife Fund works in over 100 countries to build a future in which people live in harmony with nature. www.wwf.org.

For America, the **EarthShare** network is a valuable resource for finding the most respected environmental and conservation organisations. The groups work locally, nationally and internationally to protect our health and all aspects of our environment – air, land, water and wildlife. www.earthshare.org (US).

In Australia, check out **The Australian Conservation Fund** with its exciting EarthKids info online, at www.acfonline.org.au

Also, protecting Australian oceans and wildlife is **The Australian Marine Conservation Society** at www.marineconservation.org.au

The Canadian Wildlife Federation works to conserve Canada's wildlife and habitats for the enjoyment of all. Online you'll find lots of children's resources, including a kids' channel, at www.cwf-fcf.org (Canada).

Products and suppliers

There are many ethical, eco-minded toys, clothes, nappies and other products out there; here are a few of my favourites.

Frugi offers a brilliant range of **organic clothes**. If you are using reusable nappies, Frugi love fluffy bums and all their clothes provide a little more room in the bottom area. www.welovefrugi.com (UK).

Gossypium sells gorgeous, soft, **organic cotton clothing**. My daughter had a lovely pair of their PJs which were durable too. www.gossypium.co.uk (UK).

For an innovative, easy way to give (or receive) **cloth nappies as a gift**, try a Nap Nap voucher. www.napnaphq.com (UK).

Really Eco Baby is a lovely **online shop** that takes the guess work out of choosing ethical and eco products, such as skincare, chocolate, clothes, toys and gifts. www.reallyecobaby.co.uk (UK).

Earthlings is a great supplier of 100% natural, **organic cotton clothing** for babies, toddlers and children. www.earthlings.co.nz (NZ).

I love **soapnut shells** for eco-clean washing. My favourite UK supplier can be found at www.soapnuts. co.uk. For America, try www.naturoli.com. In Australia try www.soapinanutshell.com.au and Canada, www.buysoapnuts.com.

Bambino Mio for **reusable nappies** and swim nappies. www.bambinomio.com (UK).

Myriad Natural Toys for wonderful **green toys**, books and eco-friendly art and craft materials. www.myriadonline.co.uk (UK).

EverEarth sell sustainable, attractive and durable **eco toys**. www.everearth.co.uk (UK, US and Australia).

Weleda (UK, US, Canada and Australia) for organic, sustainably sourced **skincare** for babies and the whole family, at www.weleda.com. Also consider Burt's Bees, at www.burtsbees.co.uk (UK) or www.burtsbees.com (US).

Earth Friendly Baby for gentle, organic **body washes, bubble baths and shampoos**. www.earthfriendlybaby.co.uk (UK).

For outdoors adventures with a little one, you can't beat **baby-wearing**. Two brilliant makes of versatile, safe and comfortable slings are Boba (UK, US, Australia and Canada) at www.boba.com and Je Porte Mon Bebe (UK, US, Australia and Canada) at www.jeportemonbebe.com. Before you buy, it is worth trying a few different designs at a sling library. To find one near you, try www.ukslinglibraries.wordpress.com (UK). Because most designs are fully washable, they also make a good secondhand purchase.

Index

Learning with Nature

A **how-to** guide to **inspiring children** through outdoor **games** and **activities**

Marina Robb ▪ Victoria Mew ▪ Anna Richardson

Learning with Nature is full of fun activities and games to get your children outdoors, to explore, have fun, make things and learn about nature and help them grow up happy and healthy. Suitable for groups of children aged between 3 and 16, the graded activities help children develop key practical and social skills, awareness of their place in the world, respect for the natural world, and all this while enjoying the great outdoors!

Written by experienced Forest School practitioners, using tried and tested games and activities, it provides comprehensive information for enriching childrens' learning through nature. The games and activities are clearly categorized, with step-by-step instructions, age guide, a list of resources needed, and invisible learning points.

This book is a unique must-have resource for families, schools, youth groups and anyone working with children.

green books

About Green Books

Environmental publishers for 25 years. For our full range of titles and to order direct from our website, see: www.greenbooks.co.uk

Send us a book proposal on eco-building, science, gardening, etc.: see www.greenbooks.co.uk/for-authors

For bulk orders (50+ copies) we offer discount terms. For details, contact: sales@greenbooks.co.uk

Join our mailing list for new titles, special offers, reviews and author events: www.greenbooks.co.uk/subscribe

 @ Green_Books    /GreenBooks